ALSO BY HAROLD BLOOM

SHAKESPEARE'S PERSONALITIES

FALSTAFF

GIVE ME LIFE

HAROLD BLOOM

SCRIBNER

New York   London   Toronto   Sydney   New Delhi

SCRIBNER
An Imprint of Simon & Schuster, Inc.
1230 Avenue of the Americas
New York, NY 10020

First Scribner hardcover edition April 2017

SCRIBNER and design are registered trademarks of The Gale Group, Inc.,
used under license by Simon & Schuster, Inc., the publisher of this work.

For information about special discounts for bulk purchases,
please contact Simon & Schuster Special Sales at 1-866-506-1949
or business@simonandschuster.com.

The Simon & Schuster Speakers Bureau can bring authors to your live event.
For more information or to book an event contact the Simon & Schuster Speakers
Bureau at 1-866-248-3049 or visit our website at www.simonspeakers.com.

Interior design by Erich Hobbing

Manufactured in the United States of America

1 3 5 7 9 10 8 6 4 2

Library of Congress Cataloging-in-Publication Data is available.

ISBN 978-1-5011-6413-2
ISBN 978-1-5011-6415-6 (ebook)

For F. Murray Abraham

Contents

CONTENTS

Acknowledgments

I would like to acknowledge my research assistant, Alice Kenney, and my editor, Nan Graham. As always I am indebted to my literary agents, Glen Hartley and Lynn Chu. I have a particular debt to Glen Hartley, who first suggested this sequence of five brief books on Shakespeare's personalities.

Author's Note

In the main I have followed the latest Arden edition, but have repunctuated according to my understanding of the text. In a few places, I have restored Shakespeare's language, where I judge traditional emendations to be mistaken.

FALSTAFF

GIVE ME LIFE

CHAPTER 1

Prelude

I fell in love with Sir John Falstaff when I was a boy of twelve, almost seventy-five years ago. A rather plump and melancholy youth, I turned to him out of need, because I was lonely. Finding myself in him liberated me from a debilitating self-consciousness.

He has never abandoned me for three-quarters of a century and I trust will be with me until the end. The true and perfect image of life abides with him: robustly, unforgettably, forever. He exposes what is counterfeit in me and in all others.

If Socrates had been born in Geoffrey Chaucer's England and had gone to Eastcheap, a London street, to purchase meat, he might have stopped for ale or sack at the Boar's Head Tavern. There he would have encountered Falstaff and traded wit and wisdom with him. I have not the skill to portray that imaginary meeting. Only a fusion of Aristophanes and Samuel Beckett could manage it. Decades ago, sharing Fundador with Anthony Burgess on a Manhattan evening in 1972, I suggested he would be able to venture on the task but he demurred.

A lifelong Falstaffian at eighty-six, I have come to believe that if we are to represent Shakespeare by only one play, it ought to be the complete *Henry IV*, to which I would add Mistress Quickly's description of the death of Falstaff in act 2, scene 3 of *Henry V*. I think of this as the Falstaffiad rather than the Henriad, as scholars tend to call it.

Shakespeare never surpassed the alternation between the royal

1

court, the rebels, and Eastcheap in these three plays. The transitions between high and low are so deft they seem invisible.

Is there in all Western literature a portrayal of ambivalence to match Hal/Henry V? In regard to both the King, his father, and to Hotspur, his rival, the Prince is a whirligig of contraries. Toward Falstaff his long gathering ambivalence has turned murderous. Hal's imagination is haunted by the wishful image of Sir John Falstaff on the gallows. The wretched Bardolph is hanged by his new King and former companion, in *Henry V*, without regret. Had Falstaff not departed for Arthur's bosom, Mistress Quickly's poignant mistake for Abraham's bosom, he would have dangled by Bardolph's side.

More than a few scholars of Shakespeare share Hal's ambivalence toward Falstaff. This no longer surprises me. They are the undead and Falstaff is the everliving. I wonder that the greatest wit in literature should be chastised for his vices since all of them are perfectly open and cheerfully self-acknowledged. Supreme wit is one of the highest cognitive powers. Falstaff is as intelligent as Hamlet. But Hamlet is death's ambassador while Falstaff is the embassy of life.

The heroic vitalists in literature include Rabelais' Panurge, Chaucer's Wife of Bath, and Cervantes' Sancho Panza. Falstaff reigns over them. John Ruskin taught that the only wealth is life. Sir John Falstaff, the Socrates of Eastcheap, embodies that truth.

What is the essence of Falstaffianism? My late friend and drinking companion Anthony Burgess told me it was freedom from the state. Anthony and I never quite agreed on that though indeed no societal standards ever could abide Falstaff. I recall telling Burgess that for me the essence of Falstaffianism was: *do not moralize.* Computing Falstaff's flaws is trivial: he bulges with them. Hal, like his father Bolingbroke, is the essence of hypocrisy. They are Machiavels. Bolingbroke, who becomes Henry IV, is a usurper and a regicide. His nonsensical obsession is that he will expiate the murder of Richard II by leading yet another crusade to capture Jerusalem. He dies indeed in the chamber of his palace called Jerusalem. Hal, when he becomes Henry V, leads a land grab to capture France. A crusade is what one might expect of Prince Hal, who hungers like Hotspur for what both call honor. Falstaff destroys the validity of that appetite in a reply to Hal in act 5, scene 1 in the first part of *Henry IV*:

> **Hal:** Why, thou owest God a death. [*Exit.*]
> **Falstaff:** 'Tis not due yet; I would be loath to pay him before
> his day. What need I be so forward with him that calls
> not on me? Well, 'tis no matter; honour pricks me on.
> Yea, but how if honour prick me off when I come on?
> how then? Can honour set to a leg? No: or an arm? no:
> or take away the grief of a wound? no. Honour hath no
> skill in surgery, then? no. What is honour? a word. What
> is in that word honour? what is that honour? air. A trim
> reckoning! Who hath it? he that died o' Wednesday.
> Doth he feel it? no. Doth he hear it? no. 'Tis insensible,
> then. Yea, to the dead. But will it not live with the living?
> no. Why? detraction will not suffer it. Therefore I'll
> none of it. Honour is a mere scutcheon: and so ends my
> catechism.
>
> act 5, scene 1, lines 126–40

If there could be a religion of vitalism this would do very well for its catechism. Falstaff mocks faith, killing the insane notion that we owe God our death. Knowingly he also mocks both Hal and himself. Disreputable and joyous, he speaks to a world that goes from violence to violence.

Falstaff immediately became the most popular of all Shakespearean personalities, and remains so. The audiences at the Globe and the readers who purchased quartos found little to moralize against in Sir John. His being overflows and that excess brings new meanings to our minds. Exuberance in itself is a shadowy virtue and can be dangerous to the self and to others, but in Falstaff it generates more life.

I am weary of being accused of sentimentalizing Falstaff. I once told a benign interviewer:

> Remember, there are three great poets whom neither you nor I would want to have lunch or dinner with, or even a drink— François Villon, Christopher Marlowe, and Arthur Rimbaud. At the least they would rob us, at the most they might kill us. Sir John Falstaff wouldn't kill us, but he would certainly gull us one way or another, and perhaps pick our pockets very adeptly.

In that sense the sublime Falstaff is bad news. Against myself I cite Orson Welles, whose *Chimes at Midnight* remains a neglected masterpiece. Welles made the film, an adaptation of the Henriad, and played it as tragedy. The film had a supporting cast of brilliant stars including Keith Baxter as Hal, John Gielgud as Henry IV, Jeanne Moreau as Doll Tearsheet, Margaret Rutherford as Mistress Quickly, and Ralph Richardson as the Narrator. Welles called Falstaff a "gloriously life-affirming good man . . . defending a force—the old England—which is going down. What is difficult about Falstaff . . . is that he is the greatest conception of a good man, the most completely good man, in all drama. His faults are so small and he makes tremendous jokes out of little faults. But his goodness is like bread, like wine."

I may be unique in my total agreement with Orson Welles. Is there anyone else in *Henry IV* whose goodness is like bread, like wine? They are scurvy politicians like the King and the brilliant Prince Hal and most of the rebels. They are smug thugs like Prince John and high-spirited killing machines like the captivating Hotspur and Douglas. Falstaff's followers—Bardolph, Nym, the outrageous Pistol—are entertaining rogues, and Mistress Quickly and Doll Tearsheet are better company than the Lord Chief Justice. Justice Shallow is charmingly absurd and his crony Silence augments the irreality.

Falstaff is as bewildering as Hamlet, as infinitely varied as Cleopatra. He can be apprehended but never fully comprehended. There is no end to Falstaff. His matrix is freedom but he dies for love.

Oliver Goldsmith in his "A Reverie at the Boar's Head Tavern, Eastcheap" is a beacon:

> The character of old Falstaff, even with all his faults, gives me more consolation than the most studied efforts of wisdom. I here behold an agreeable old fellow, forgetting age, and showing me the way to be young at sixty-five. Sure I am well able to be as merry, though not so comical as he. Is it not in my power to have, though not so much wit, at least as much vivacity? Age, care, wisdom, reflection, begone! I give you to the winds. Let's have t'other bottle; here's to the memory of Shakespeare, Falstaff, and all the merry men of Eastcheap!

Falstaff is possibly closer to seventy-five than sixty-five. Dr. Samuel Johnson, who discovered and fostered Goldsmith, similarly celebrated Falstaff while expressing moral disapproval. Maurice Morgann is the true ancestor of all Falstaffians. His *An Essay on the Dramatic Character of Sir John Falstaff*, published in 1777, was criticized by Johnson, who facetiously suggested Morgann should next try to prove Iago a good man. The issue was the supposed cowardice of the Fat Knight. It is an accusation first made by Prince Hal, who fiercely needs to persuade Falstaff to confess his cowardice. Why?

Crossing the threshold to the sinuous consciousness of Hal/ Henry V, second King of the Lancaster line, we confront the wavering presence of ontology itself, the immanence of Sir John Falstaff. Why did Shakespeare invent Falstaff?

Literary character is always an invention and indebted to prior inventions. Shakespeare invented literary character as we know it. He reformed our expectations for the verbal imitation of personality and the reformation appears to be permanent and uncannily inevitable. The Bible and Homer powerfully render personages yet their characters are mostly unchanging. They age and die within their stories but their modes of being do not develop.

Shakespeare's personalities do. The representation of character in his plays now seems normative and indeed became the accepted mode almost immediately. Shakespeare's personalities have little in common with those of Ben Jonson or Christopher Marlowe. Shakespeare's originality in portraying women and men founds itself upon *The Canterbury Tales* of Geoffrey Chaucer.

Throughout Shakespeare, vitality transmutes into doom-eagerness. Richard II, the protagonist of the history that begins the Henriad, is a moral masochist whose luxurious self-indulgence in despair augments his overthrow by the usurper Bolingbroke, who thus becomes Henry IV. In the personality of Richard II, Shakespeare prefigures that element in all of us by which we render bad situations even worse through our own hyperbolic language.

Falstaff is different. His zest for life pervades his torrent of language and laughter. Hotspur is the incarnation of doom-eagerness. His mode though is opposite to that of Richard II. His vaunting language assaults the frontiers of what is possible. Hal, his father's son, distrusts his own vitalism, and yet goes to Falstaff to be confirmed in it. The royal pupil proves unforgiving toward his teacher.

Kings have no friends, only followers, and Sir John Falstaff is no man's follower.

Directors, actors, playgoers, readers need to understand that Falstaff, most magnificent of wits, is tragicomic. Unlike Hotspur and Hal, he is not one of the fools of time. Dr. Johnson said that love was the wisdom of fools, and the folly of the wise. I cannot think of a better description of my hero Sir John Falstaff.

CHAPTER 2

Playing Falstaff

I first performed the role of Falstaff on the evening of October 30, 2000, with the American Repertory Theater in Cambridge, Massachusetts. Robert Brustein, who then headed the ART, played ancient Pistol, Will Lebow did a number of parts including Bardolph, while Thomas Derrah was Hal and Karen MacDonald, Mistress Quickly, and I was Falstaff. The director Karin Coonrod and I prepared a text drawn from the two parts of *Henry IV* and Mistress Quickly's lament for Falstaff in act 2, scene 3 of *Henry V*.

I composed an epilogue to what I had named the Falstaffiad and echoed Shakespeare's language as best I could:

Nay sure I am not in Hell; I am in Arthur's bosom. And yet I am but the counterfeit shadow of Sir John Falstaff, since I have not the life of a man. Here there is honor, and no vanity, but no time at all to jest and dally. Water aplenty, but no sherris-sack; there is no blood to warm. My voice is broken, with all this hallowing and singing of anthems.

Where are Bardolph and Pistol and mine Hostess of the Tavern? Where is Doll?

I was old in judgement and understanding, but young enough while I lived, and I offended only the virtuous. Now I want your excellent sherris-sack to illumine my face, which as a beacon again would give warning to all the rest of this little kingdom, man, to arm. Yet I dream; I am in Arthur's bosom, and so grant me your farewell.

I read the role again at the Yale British Art Center, again directed by Karin Coonrod with the young Michael Stuhlbarg as Hal. I recall also a few scattered enactments as Falstaff for the Shakespeare Society for New York City.

I have seen two magnificent portrayals of Falstaff. The first was the major theatrical experience of my life. On the evenings of May 7 and 8, 1946, I attended the Century Theater in New York City to watch the Old Vic of London put on *Henry IV, Part 1* and the next night *Part 2*. Ralph Richardson, who seems to me the supreme actor of my lifetime, was Falstaff. Laurence Olivier was Hotspur the first evening, and with amazing versatility Justice Shallow the second.

Richardson did not play Falstaff as comedy. The wealth of his interpretation is difficult to convey. A wounded dignity was fused with daemonic energy, deep wisdom, and an even more profound melancholy. Pride was uppermost and necessarily had to be degraded. The effect bordered upon tragedy yet resolutely would not cross all the way into it, as Orson Welles did with his tragedy of Sir John Falstaff.

Were I an actor, I might try to imitate both Richardson and Welles. Their Falstaff was no coward but a realist. He would fight only so long as he saw reason. He was *homo ludens* who valued the order of play. For him all was fiction save in games. Falstaff is most delighted and delightful when he acts out skits with Hal. On the battlefield he scorns carnage, sensibly wishes he was back at the Boar's Head Tavern, carries a bottle of sack in his holster, and regards death and dying as bad jests. Who can resist a veteran warrior who has seen through the absurdity of violence and urges us to play instead?

Shakespeare explores the paradox that Falstaff, like Hamlet, seems an actual person placed on stage surrounded by actors. In the presence of Sir John Falstaff even Hal and Hotspur are only shadows. Hamlet is ringed by shadows who waver as Claudius, Gertrude, Ophelia, and are no more substantial than the ghost of the slain father.

To be Falstaff is to assault the frontiers between seeming and being. Falstaff is no everyman, since like Hamlet his cognitive reach is immense. But all of us, whatever our age or gender, participate in him.

Falstaff wants us to love him. Hamlet does not need or want our love. The tragedy of Falstaff stems from his fear of rejection. Who among us does not dread being rejected and cast out by those we love?

The ultimate difficulty in acting Falstaff is that he is too large in every sense to stay within even the ambience of the *Henry IV* plays. Like Hamlet, he walks off the stage into the realm of our lives. William Hazlitt remarked: "It is we who are Hamlet." We cannot say that we are Falstaff though when I was younger and less weary I dallied with being Falstaff.

Falstaff brooks no rebuttal. His cascade of language blooms into a glowing radiance. He is the custodian of Shakespeare's word hoard. Ralph Richardson and Orson Welles in different ways expressed the eloquent extravagances of the Falstaffian modes. Richardson made love to every word, rolling each to its limits. Welles relished the goodness of every phrase, tasting it as if it were bread and wine.

In 1951, in London I saw Anthony Quayle as Falstaff, with Michael Redgrave as Hotspur, Richard Burton as Prince Hal, and Harry Andrews as Henry IV. Quayle was an extraordinary actor but his Falstaff was harsh and one wondered how this could be a useful interpretation. Much better was Paul Rogers, whom I saw in London in May 1955, where the knowing precariousness of Falstaff's relation to Hal was emphasized.

I saw neither Kevin Kline nor Antony Sher play Sir John on stage but there will be actors playing Falstaff as long as there are humans on Earth. And I go on rereading, teaching, and meditating upon his magnificence.

CHAPTER 3

Beautiful, Laughing, Living Speech

William Butler Yeats gave us the perfect phrase for the way Falstaff speaks:

> If one has not fine construction, one has not drama, but if one has not beautiful or powerful and individual speech, one has not literature, or, at any rate, one has not great literature. Rabelais, Villon, Shakespeare, William Blake, would have known one another by their speech. Some of them knew how to construct a story, but all of them had abundant, resonant, beautiful, laughing, living speech.

To place Shakespeare with Rabelais, Villon, Blake is to enter with many of his major personalities into the company of heroic vitalists. When we listen to Falstaff, we are inundated by abundance and resonance and are seduced by the beauty of his laughter and his vitalizing diction.

Begin with act 1, scene 2 of *Henry IV, Part 1*:

Falstaff: Now, Hal, what time of day is it, lad?
Hal: Thou art so fat-witted, with drinking of old sack and
    unbuttoning thee after supper and sleeping upon
    benches after noon, that thou hast forgotten to demand

that truly which thou wouldst truly know. What a devil hast thou to do with the time of the day? Unless hours were cups of sack and minutes capons and clocks the tongues of bawds and dials the signs of leaping-houses and the blessèd sun himself a fair hot wench in flame-coloured taffeta, I see no reason why thou shouldst be so superfluous to demand the time of the day.

Falstaff: Indeed, you come near me now, Hal; for we that take purses go by the moon and the seven stars, and not by Phoebus, he, 'that wandering knight so fair.' And, I prithee, sweet wag, when thou art king, as, God save thy grace,— majesty I should say, for grace thou wilt have none,—

Hal: What, none?

Falstaff: No, by my troth, not so much as will serve to prologue to an egg and butter.

Hal: Well, how then? come, roundly, roundly.

Falstaff: Marry, then, sweet wag, when thou art king, let not us that are squires of the night's body be called thieves of the day's beauty: let us be Diana's foresters, gentlemen of the shade, minions of the moon; and let men say we be men of good government, being governed, as the sea is, by our noble and chaste mistress the moon, under whose countenance we steal.

Hal: Thou sayest well, and it holds well too; for the fortune of us that are the moon's men doth ebb and flow like the sea, being governed, as the sea is, by the moon. As, for proof, now: a purse of gold most resolutely snatched on Monday night and most dissolutely spent on Tuesday morning; got with swearing 'Lay by' and spent with crying 'Bring in;' now in as low an ebb as the foot of the ladder and by and by in as high a flow as the ridge of the gallows.

act 1, scene 2, lines 1–37

Hal and Falstaff enter from opposite sides of the stage with Sir John rubbing his eyes as he emerges from the heavy sleep of much sack (a rawer version of what we now call a heavy oloroso). In Falstaff's presence others emulate him, including Hal, speaking prose in his style and cadence. Not only witty in himself but the cause of wit in other men, Falstaff contaminates the language of any speaker much in his presence.

Sir John's amiable question, "Now, Hal, what time of day is it?" is answered by a torrent of vehemence clearly learned from Falstaff's own instruction. I wince at Hal's high-spirited rancor but forgive him for the brilliance of his delicious vision of the blessed sun as a fair hot wench in flame-colored taffeta. Even at eighty-six I kindle at the thought of a comely wench in a bright red silk dress. Falstaff recovers instantly with his audacious request that in the reign of Henry V, highwaymen like himself will be gentlemen of the shade governed by the moon under whose countenance they steal.

Together Falstaff and Hal soon mount into what I regard as the Falstaffian Sublime:

> **Falstaff:** Thou hast the most unsavoury similes and art indeed the most comparative, rascalliest, sweet young prince. But, Hal, I prithee, trouble me no more with vanity. I would to God thou and I knew where a commodity of good names were to be bought. An old lord of the Council rated me the other day in the street about you, sir, but I marked him not; and yet he talked very wisely, but I regarded him not; and yet he talked wisely, and in the street too.
>
> **Hal:** Thou didst well, for wisdom cries out in the streets, and no man regards it.
>
> **Falstaff:** O, thou hast damnable iteration and art indeed able to corrupt a saint. Thou hast done much harm upon me,

Hal; God forgive thee for it. Before I knew thee, Hal,
I knew nothing, and now am I, if a man should speak
truly, little better than one of the wicked. I must give
over this life, and I will give it over. By the Lord, and I
do not, I am a villain. I'll be damned for never a king's
son in Christendom.

act 1, scene 2, lines 76–94

"Vanity" is a conflagration perpetually poised to break out in
the friction between Falstaff and Hal. Vanity is a mistranslation
of the Hebrew *hevel*, which is a mere "vapor," a "breath," and so
finally nothingness. When Hal pillories Falstaff for his supposed
vanity, the lambasting is murderous. I wonder often whether God
will forgive Henry V for the harm he finally inflicts upon Sir
John.

The Prince's darkly witty rejoinder to Falstaff's joyous parody
alludes to a superb text:

Wisdom crieth without; she uttereth her voice in the streets:
    She crieth in the chief place of concourse, in the openings of
the gates: in the city she uttereth her words, saying,
    How long, ye simple ones, will ye love simplicity? and the
scorners delight in their scorning, and fools hate knowledge?
    Turn you at my reproof: behold, I will pour out my spirit
unto you, I will make known my words unto you.
    Because I have called, and ye refused; I have stretched out my
hand, and no man regarded.

Proverbs 1: 20–24

Unyielding in my passion for Falstaff, I have a particular regard
for his riposte:

O, thou hast damnable iteration and art indeed able to corrupt a saint. Thou hast done much harm upon me, Hal; God forgive thee for it! Before I knew thee, Hal, I knew nothing, and now am I, if a man should speak truly, little better than one of the wicked. I must give over this life, and I will give it over: by the Lord, and I do not, I am a villain: I'll be damned for never a king's son in Christendom.

act 1, scene 2, lines 87–94

Feigning a Puritan piety, Sir John castigates Hal for his blasphemous twisting of a religious text and associates himself with the godly. When I was younger, I enjoyed applying Falstaff's wit by remarking to one friend or another that before I knew them, I knew nothing, and now am I, if Bloom should speak truly, little better than one of the wicked. I gave this up because it began to shadow friendship, yet I recall it with nostalgia.

When Falstaff departs for Eastcheap Hal and his accomplice Poins plot to disguise themselves and attack Sir John and three underlings after a highway robbery. I am fascinated when Hal bids Falstaff be gone: "Farewell, the latter spring; farewell, All-hallown summer." I do not think Hal means that Falstaff is a very old man behaving like an adolescent. Rather Falstaff is Indian summer following after Hallowe'en. It is as though, for one startling moment, a trace of earlier affection revives. Yet soon this totally dissipates:

> I know you all, and will awhile uphold
> The unyoked humour of your idleness.
> Yet herein will I imitate the sun,
> Who doth permit the base contagious clouds
> To smother up his beauty from the world,
> That, when he please again to be himself,

Being wanted, he may be more wondered at
By breaking through the foul and ugly mists
Of vapours that did seem to strangle him.
If all the year were playing holidays,
To sport would be as tedious as to work;
But when they seldom come, they wished-for come,
And nothing pleaseth but rare accidents.
So, when this loose behaviour I throw off
And pay the debt I never promised,
By how much better than my word I am,
By so much shall I falsify men's hopes;
And, like bright metal on a sullen ground,
My reformation, glittering o'er my fault,
Shall show more goodly and attract more eyes
Than that which hath no foil to set it off.
I'll so offend to make offence a skill,
Redeeming time when men think least I will.

act 1, scene 2, lines 185–207

What are we to make of this abrupt movement into verse solil-oquy? My hero Samuel Johnson nods and calls it "a great mind offering excuses to itself." The brilliance of the speech is beyond question. I recite it and remember William Hazlitt's characteriza-tion of Henry V as "a very amiable monster, a very splendid pag-eant." Of Falstaff, Hazlitt remarked in *Characters of Shakespeare's Plays*: "He keeps up perpetual holiday and open house, and we live with him in a round, of invitations to a rump and dozen."

I suppose Hal's soliloquy is skillful enough if you like that sort of thing. Perhaps it should be adopted by schools of organization and management as a manual for self-advancement. Has it poetic value? Shakespeare is the greatest of perspectivists. Confronting his personalities we see and hear only what we are until he has taught us to go beyond our limits. Shift perspectives and we come to realize that Hal is his father's son. Royal father and royal son have made offence a skill. But they do it very differently. Richard II, whom Henry IV deposed and then had murdered in prison, bitterly reflected: "I wasted time, and now doth time waste me"; Henry IV never wasted time. Hal's Machiavellian soliloquy presumes a tidy division of sport versus work. Does that redeem time? Falstaff, who glories in the unproductive, and exalts play, brushes time aside and bids it pass.

CHAPTER 4

Hotspur:
Die All, Die Merrily

The vexed relationship between Hal and Falstaff is the center of the *Henry IV* plays. Hal's rival Hotspur might be called the alternative fulcrum of *Henry IV, Part 1*. Hotspur is Henry Percy, the son of the Earl of Northumberland, who had been crucial in Henry IV's rise to power. The role of Hotspur is both a contrast to Hal's and a prophecy of what will become Hal's mission, to vindicate Henry IV's legitimacy. Hotspur's vision of honor is precisely opposite to Falstaff's:

> By heaven, methinks it were an easy leap
> To pluck bright honour from the pale-faced moon,
> Or dive into the bottom of the deep,
> Where fathom-line could never touch the ground,
> And pluck up drowned honour by the locks;
> So he that doth redeem her thence might wear
> Without corrival, all her dignities:
> But out upon this half-faced fellowship!
>
> act 1, scene 3, lines 200–207

For Hotspur, as for Hal, honor is an accolade in the particular sense of the touch that confers knighthood. Hotspur verges just short of parody in the ferocity of his drive to achieve by destruc-

21

tion. Remembering Laurence Olivier as Hotspur compels me to be charmed unwillingly when this warlord of the North cries out in response to a letter holding back from armed rebellion: "'The purpose you undertake is dangerous;'—why, that's certain: 'tis dangerous to take a cold, to sleep, to drink; but I tell you, my lord fool, out of this nettle, danger, we pluck this flower, safety."

Hotspur's eloquence is singular. A vaunting spirit, he is a throwback to an illusory age of chivalry, but his flights are tempered by a wit just this side of irony:

Glendower: Sit, cousin Percy.
        Sit, good cousin Hotspur, for by that name,
        As oft as Lancaster doth speak of you,
        His cheek looks pale and with a rising sigh
        He wisheth you in heaven.
Hotspur: And you in hell
        As oft as he hears Owen Glendower spoke of.
Glendower: I cannot blame him. At my nativity
        The front of heaven was full of fiery shapes,
        Of burning cressets; and at my birth
        The frame and huge foundation of the earth
        Shaked like a coward.
Hotspur: Why, so it would have done at the same season, if
        your mother's cat had but kittened, though yourself had
        never been born.
Glendower: I say the earth did shake when I was born.
Hotspur: And I say the earth was not of my mind,
        If you suppose as fearing you it shook.
Glendower: The heavens were all on fire, the earth did
        tremble.
Hotspur: O, then the earth shook to see the heavens on fire,
        And not in fear of your nativity.

Diseased nature oftentimes breaks forth
In strange eruptions; oft the teeming earth
Is with a kind of colic pinched and vexed
By the imprisoning of unruly wind
Within her womb; which, for enlargement striving,
Shakes the old beldam earth and topples down
Steeples and moss-grown towers. At your birth
Our grandam earth, having this distemperature,
In passion shook.

act 3, scene 1, lines 6–34

Glendower's wild and whirling rhetoric entertains by its boasting yet is repetitious and redundant. Think back to Falstaff's supple blandishments where each word is honeyed and a fine excess beguiles us. Hal, parrying Falstaff, mocks the master with his own grandiloquence. Hotspur carries the audience by English plainspokenness opposing Welsh grandiosity.

Glendower: Cousin, of many men
I do not bear these crossings. Give me leave
To tell you once again that at my birth
The front of heaven was full of fiery shapes,
The goats ran from the mountains, and the herds
Were strangely clamorous to the frighted fields.
These signs have marked me extraordinary;
And all the courses of my life do show
I am not in the roll of common men.
Where is he living, clipped in with the sea
That chides the banks of England, Scotland, Wales,
Which calls me pupil, or hath read to me?
And bring him out that is but woman's son
Can trace me in the tedious ways of art

And hold me pace in deep experiments.

Hotspur: I think there's no man speaks better Welsh.
I'll to dinner.

Mortimer: Peace, cousin Percy; you will make him mad.

Glendower: I can call spirits from the vasty deep.

Hotspur: Why, so can I, or so can any man,
But will they come when you do call for them?

Glendower: Why, I can teach you, cousin, to command the
devil.

Hotspur: And I can teach thee, coz, to shame the devil:
By telling truth: 'Tell truth and shame the devil.'
If thou have power to raise him, bring him hither,
And I'll be sworn I have power to shame him hence.
O, while you live, 'tell truth and shame the devil.'

act 3, scene 1, lines 34–60

Hotspur charms us with his dry: "I think there's no man speaks better Welsh. / I'll to dinner." Glendower again roars his preter-natural powers: "I can call spirits from the vasty deep." To which Hotspur delivers a crushing response:

Why, so can I, or so can any man,
But will they come when you do call for them?

The defeat and death of Hotspur enlarges our empathic response to his vehement quest for glory. With truncated forces, he must battle the entire royal army. His response to Hal's new guise as warrior is fiery:

No more, no more: worse than the sun in March
This praise doth nourish agues. Let them come!

They come like sacrifices in their trim,
And to the fire-eyed maid of smoky war
All hot and bleeding will we offer them.
The mailed Mars shall on his altar sit
Up to the ears in blood. I am on fire
To hear this rich reprisal is so nigh
And yet not ours. Come, let me taste my horse,
Who is to bear me like a thunderbolt
Against the bosom of the Prince of Wales:
Harry to Harry shall, hot horse to horse,
Meet and ne'er part till one drop down a corpse.

act 4, scene 1, lines 110–22

When told that Henry IV's army is thirty thousand strong, Hotspur is defiant and on another level resigned:

Forty let it be.
My father and Glendower being both away,
The powers of us may serve so great a day.
Come, let us take a muster speedily.
Doomsday is near. Die all, die merrily.

act 4, scene 1, lines 129–33

It is inadequate to interpret this sentence as "if we must die, let's do it cheerfully." That demeans Hotspur's courage never to submit nor yield. Doomsday to him is neither the last judgment nor a tragic event. To die merrily is to be fulfilled when the accolade was truly earned.

A Falstaffian to my deep heart's core, nevertheless I have to admire Hotspur for his verve, high spirits, and his nonchalance in throwing himself away. Shakespeare has made him much more than another killing-machine, like the Earl of Douglas. Yet who can prefer "Die all, die merrily" to Falstaff's "Give me life"?

In so far as *Henry IV, Part 1* is a component of the three-play Henriad, then its climax is the death duel between Hotspur and Hal:

> Hotspur: If I mistake not, thou art Harry Monmouth.
> Hal: Thou speak'st as if I would deny my name.
> Hotspur: My name is Harry Percy.
> Hal: Why, then I see
>   A very valiant rebel of the name.
>   I am the Prince of Wales, and think not, Percy,
>   To share with me in glory any more.
>   Two stars keep not their motion in one sphere,
>   Nor can one England brook a double reign
>   Of Harry Percy and the Prince of Wales.
> Hotspur: Nor shall it, Harry, for the hour is come
>   To end the one of us, and would to God
>   Thy name in arms were now as great as mine.
> Hal: I'll make it greater ere I part from thee,
>   And all the budding honours on thy crest
>   I'll crop, to make a garland for my head.
> Hotspur: I can no longer brook thy vanities.
> [*They fight.*]
>
> act 5, scene 4, lines 58–73

"Vanities," Hal's perpetual reproach of Falstaff, is ironically taken up by Hotspur. Shakespeare plays variations upon "vanity" throughout the Henriad, yet he intimates a preference for Falstaff's stance. When Falstaff enters to observe and cheer on Hal, he is assaulted by the formidable Earl of Douglas. Falstaff fights back and then wisely falls down as if he were dead. Douglas dashes off even as Hal destroys Hotspur:

> **Hotspur:** O, Harry, thou hast robbed me of my youth.
> I better brook the loss of brittle life
> Than those proud titles thou hast won of me.
> They wound my thoughts worse than thy sword my flesh.
> But thought's the slave of life, and life, time's fool,
> And time, that takes survey of all the world,
> Must have a stop. O, I could prophesy,
> But that the earthy and cold hand of death
> Lies on my tongue. No, Percy, thou art dust
> And food for— [*He dies.*]
>
> act 5, scene 4, lines 76–85

The complex nature of Hal appears in his tribute to Hotspur, which is then diminished by the hardly merited "ignominy," since that means only that Hotspur died attempting to usurp the usurper, Henry IV:

> **Hal:** For worms, brave Percy. Fare thee well, great heart.
> Ill-weaved ambition, how much art thou shrunk!
> When that this body did contain a spirit
> A kingdom for it was too small a bound,
> But now two paces of the vilest earth
> Is room enough. This earth that bears thee dead
> Bears not alive so stout a gentleman.
> If thou wert sensible of courtesy
> I should not make so dear a show of zeal.
> But let my favours hide thy mangled face,
> And, even in thy behalf, I'll thank myself

For doing these fair rites of tenderness.
Adieu, and take thy praise with thee to heaven.
Thy ignominy sleep with thee in the grave
But not remembered in thy epitaph.

act 5, scene 4, lines 86–100

Hotspur's unfinished final utterance is one with his heroic life. Life is the victim or fool of time from the perspective of Hotspur and of Hal. That is not at all true for Sir John Falstaff. Time must have a stop unless you thrust it aside and bid it pass. Shakespeare does not choose between Hotspur and Falstaff. You must choose.

CHAPTER 5

Whose Falstaff Is It?

There is no single Falstaff. But then we cannot say there is one Hamlet and one Hamlet only. Notoriously there are as many Hamlets as there are readers, playgoers, directors, actors, and critics. I have taught Shakespeare every semester for the last half century and more. Hamlet changes every time I reread and discuss him with my students.

In my youth and middle years I thought I knew Falstaff. That Falstaff has vanished from me. The better I know Sir John the less I know him. He has become one of the lost vehemences my midnights hold.

What makes us free? What makes me free is the capaciousness of Shakespeare's soul. He is the knowledge of what we were and of what we have become. In Balzac's novella *Louis Lambert* there is a Falstaffian cry of the human:

> Resurrection is accomplished by the wind of heaven that sweeps the worlds. The Angel carried by the wind does not say: Arise ye dead! He says: Let the living arise!

The resurrection of Sir John Falstaff takes place in one sense when he rises from his feigned corpse in the Battle of Shrewsbury. In a larger sense, Falstaff is resurrected perpetually. We read him and he springs to life.

First Falstaff is resurrected and then he dies. His resurrection begins at the joyous center of *Henry IV, Part 1*, the play within the play of act 2, scene 4, lines 356–86 when Hal and Falstaff rehearse the coming confrontation between the Prince and King Henry IV:

> **Falstaff:** But tell me, Hal, art not thou horrible afeard? thou being heir-apparent, could the world pick thee out three such enemies again as that fiend Douglas, that spirit Percy, and that devil Glendower? Art thou not horribly afraid? doth not thy blood thrill at it?
>
> **Hal:** Not a whit, i' faith; I lack some of thy instinct.
>
> **Falstaff:** Well, thou wilt be horribly chid tomorrow when thou comest to thy father: if thou love me, practise an answer.
>
> **Hal:** Do thou stand for my father, and examine me upon the particulars of my life.
>
> **Falstaff:** Shall I? content: this chair shall be my state, this dagger my sceptre, and this cushion my crown.
>
> **Hal:** Thy state is taken for a joined-stool, thy golden sceptre for a leaden dagger, and thy precious rich crown for a pitiful bald crown!
>
> **Falstaff:** Well, an the fire of grace be not quite out of thee, now shalt thou be moved. Give me a cup of sack to make my eyes look red, that it may be thought I have wept; for I must speak in passion, and I will do it in King Cambyses' vein.
>
> **Hal:** Well, here is my leg.
>
> **Falstaff:** And here is my speech. Stand aside, nobility.
>
> **Mistress Quickly:** O Jesu, this is excellent sport, i' faith!
>
> **Falstaff:** Weep not, sweet queen; for trickling tears are vain.
>
> **Hostess:** O, the father, how he holds his countenance!
>
> **Falstaff:** For God's sake, lords, convey my tristful queen; For tears do stop the flood-gates of her eyes.

Hostess: O Jesu, he doth it as like one of these harlotry players
as ever I see!

Hal inaugurates the "skit," a term not available to Shakespeare
since there are no recorded uses of it before 1727. He might have
liked the word; it has no origin and parodic overtones. What
ensues between Hal and Falstaff is far beyond parody. For Falstaff
it is joyous sport; for Hal it is malevolent:

Falstaff: Peace, good pint-pot; peace, good tickle-brain.
  Harry, I do not only marvel where thou spendest thy
  time, but also how thou art accompanied: for though
  the camomile, the more it is trodden on the faster it
  grows, yet youth, the more it is wasted the sooner it
  wears. That thou art my son, I have partly thy mother's
  word, partly my own opinion, but chiefly a villainous
  trick of thine eye and a foolish-hanging of thy nether
  lip, that doth warrant me. If then thou be son to me,
  here lies the point; why, being son to me, art thou so
  pointed at? Shall the blessed sun of heaven prove a
  micher and eat blackberries? a question not to be asked.
  Shall the son of England prove a thief and take purses?
  a question to be asked. There is a thing, Harry, which
  thou hast often heard of and it is known to many in
  our land by the name of pitch: this pitch, as ancient
  writers do report, doth defile; so doth the company thou
  keepest: for, Harry, now I do not speak to thee in drink
  but in tears, not in pleasure but in passion, not in words
  only, but in woes also: and yet there is a virtuous man
  whom I have often noted in thy company, but I know
  not his name.
Hal: What manner of man, an it like your majesty?

Falstaff: A goodly portly man, i' faith, and a corpulent; of a
cheerful look, a pleasing eye and a most noble carriage;
and, as I think, his age some fifty, or, by'r lady, inclining
to three score; and now I remember me, his name is
Falstaff: if that man should be lewdly given, he deceiveth
me; for, Harry, I see virtue in his looks. If then the tree
may be known by the fruit, as the fruit by the tree, then,
peremptorily I speak it, there is virtue in that Falstaff:
him keep with, the rest banish. And tell me now, thou
naughty varlet, tell me, where hast thou been this
month?

act 2, scene 4, 387–420

Falstaff's wistful self-portrait is poignant since it suggests his
forlorn wish that he somehow could be a father to Hal. That long-
ing has in it the seed of self-destruction.

We expect that Falstaff who personifies play should exult as
an actor. He is the master of improvisational theater. I fantasize
sometimes that he is on stage performing Samuel Beckett. When
Falstaff is bombastic in his jubilance he may be uneasily aware that
the Passion of Sir John Falstaff has commenced and will conclude
in *Henry V* with his brokenhearted death. Cast aside your sorrow
for his end and enjoy Falstaff in his prime.

W. H. Auden stayed overnight at my house just once and we
had our usual amiable disagreements on poetry since he had little use for Shelley, Whitman, and Stevens. On Falstaff, he and I
were more often in agreement, and I recall his saying that he pre-
ferred Verdi's Falstaff to Shakespeare's yet thought Sir John was
closer to redemption than all but a few other people in the plays.
I replied that Falstaff courted and accepted the obliteration of
rejection.

Falstaff, as King Henry, parodies John Lyly, a contemporary playwright with a fantastic style:

> Harry, I do not only marvel where thou spendest thy time, but also how thou art accompanied: for though the camomile, the more it is trodden on the faster it grows, yet youth, the more it is wasted the sooner it wears.
>
> act 2, scene 4, lines 389–92

That is rather more memorable than Lyly:

> Though the camomill, the more it is trodden and pressed downe, the more it spreadeth, yet the violet the oftner it is handled and touched, the sooner it withereth and decayeth . . .

Lyly is again derided in Falstaff's intricate allusion to Ecclesiasticus 13:1:

> He that toucheth pitch shall be defiled therewith; and he that hath fellowship with a proud man shall be like unto him.

Lyly had quoted this but without Falstaff's self-admonition against fellowship with a proud prince. It is delicious that Falstaff suddenly breaks into an outrageous paean of self-praise:

> A goodly portly man, i' faith, and a corpulent; of a cheerful look, a pleasing eye and a most noble carriage; and, as I think, his age some fifty, or, by'r lady, inclining to three score; and now I remember me, his name is Falstaff: if that man should be lewdly given, he deceiveth me; for, Harry, I see virtue in his looks. If then the tree may be known by the fruit, as the fruit by the tree,

then, peremptorily I speak it, there is virtue in that Falstaff: him keep with, the rest banish.

The likely age is the early seventies and Sir John is indeed lewdly given. No one in the *Henry IV* plays is virtuous in any sense whatsoever. It hardly seems to me a Shakespearean imagining. Pleased by his own performance, Falstaff indulges himself by a descent into the vernacular with: "And tell me now, thou naughty varlet, tell me, where hast thou been this month?"

Provoked, Hal reverses the roles. Falstaff becomes Hal and the Prince becomes the King. Joyously Sir John declares that he will surpass himself playing Hal. What descends upon him is an avalanche of fury and repressed violence:

Swearest thou, ungracious boy? henceforth ne'er look on me. Thou art violently carried away from grace: there is a devil haunts thee in the likeness of an old fat man; a tun of man is thy companion. Why dost thou converse with that trunk of humours, that bolting-hutch of beastliness, that swollen parcel of dropsies, that huge bombard of sack, that stuffed cloak-bag of guts, that roasted Manningtree ox with the pudding in his belly, that reverend vice, that grey iniquity, that father ruffian, that vanity in years? Wherein is he good, but to taste sack and drink it? Wherein neat and cleanly, but to carve a capon and eat it? Wherein cunning, but in craft? Wherein crafty, but in villainy? Wherein villainous, but in all things? Wherein worthy, but in nothing?

act 2, scene 4, lines 433–47

Those "that"s are stabbing, brutal, depersonalizing. The tenfold crescendo of invective demonstrates how well the Prince has learned the lesson of the Master. There is a progressive leap from metaphor to damnation in the movement from a trunk of humors or diseases to a trough of beastliness and then on to a parcel of plagues, a vat of oloroso, a suitcase of intestines, and best of all, a whole roasted ox with a pudding in his belly. Real nastiness takes over with the Reverend Vice, the gray-haired sin of favoritism, the aged swaggerer, and inevitably vanity.

Hal is less creative accusing Falstaff of villainy or moral turpitude. Having yet more power to hurt, the Prince abandons his rank and for once loses control:

> Falstaff: I would your grace would take me with you. Whom
> means your grace?
> Hal: That villainous abominable misleader of youth, Falstaff,
> that old white-bearded Satan.
> Falstaff: My lord, the man I know.
> Hal: I know thou dost.
> Falstaff: But to say I know more harm in him than in myself,
> were to say more than I know. That he is old, the more
> the pity, his white hairs do witness it; but that he is,
> saving your reverence, a whoremaster, that I utterly
> deny. If sack and sugar be a fault, God help the wicked!
> if to be old and merry be a sin, then many an old host
> that I know is damned: if to be fat be to be hated, then
> Pharaoh's lean kine are to be loved. No, my good lord;
> banish Peto, banish Bardolph, banish Poins: but for
> sweet Jack Falstaff, kind Jack Falstaff, true Jack Falstaff,
> valiant Jack Falstaff, and therefore more valiant, being,
> as he is, old Jack Falstaff, banish not him thy Harry's
> company, banish not him thy Harry's company: banish
> plump Jack, and banish all the world.
>   act 2, scene 4, lines 448–67

Falstaff defends himself as a life force, dropping "Sir" and being only "Jack." He warns Hal that to banish plump Jack is to banish all the world that is not politics and violence. A universe of play will vanish forever. But with remorseless intensity, the Prince dismisses his teacher:

Hal: I do, I will.

act 2, scene 4, line 468

With pained dignity, Sir John declines to understand and provokes Hal to a shout of outrage: "That villainous abominable misleader of youth, Falstaff, that old white-bearded Satan." If the Prince is a misled youth then Sir John is both a Lucifer hoary with age and a Socrates set up for execution. Falstaff is a perpetual freshness. He is no Satan but an aged morning and evening star. To destroy the teacher is to execute Socrates. Even Falstaff surpasses expectation with the fable of Pharaoh's lean kine:

And it came to pass at the end of two full years, that Pharaoh dreamed: and, behold, he stood by the river.

And, behold, there came up out of the river seven well favoured kine and fatfleshed; and they fed in a meadow.

And, behold, seven other kine came up after them out of the river, ill favoured and leanfleshed; and stood by the other kine upon the brink of the river.

And the ill favoured and leanfleshed kine did eat up the seven well favoured and fat kine. So Pharaoh awoke.

Genesis 41:1–4

Joseph the Provider read this as seven years of abundance followed by seven of dearth. No defense of vitality and appetite matches this.

More than a decade older than Falstaff, I value him more since it is not easy to be old and merry. I emerged just now from three hard days in which I have been sullen in the sweet air. Sir John cures me. Is he not sweet, kind, and true? As for valor, if you take it to be audacity, age has not withered nor custom staled Falstaff's infinite vitality. If you are a moldy fig or a bossy handshaker, then you are happy to banish Sir John. Many of us belong to the company whose motto is: Banish plump Jack, and banish all the world.

The loud knocking at the door heightens Falstaff's dread of banishment and Hal's grimly resolute "I do, I will."

The Prince has more than banishment in mind; something in him wants to see Falstaff hanged. Sir John shows true valor in disdaining the sheriff and watchman waiting to arrest him for the capital offense of highway robbery. To Bardolph's anguished warning, Falstaff zestfully calls out: "Out, ye rogue! Play out the play: I have much to say in the behalf of that Falstaff."

The moment of crisis is here. If Hal tells Mistress Quickly to admit the sheriff and his watch then Falstaff swings. The Prince is a double man and a counterfeit. Falstaff is Falstaff and a true piece of gold:

> **Falstaff:** Dost thou hear, Hal? never call a true piece of gold a
> counterfeit: thou art essentially mad without seeming so.
> **Hal:** And thou a natural coward without instinct.
> **Falstaff:** I deny your major. If you will deny the sheriff, so;
> if not, let him enter: if I become not a cart as well as
> another man, a plague on my bringing up! I hope I shall
> as soon be strangled with a halter as another.
> **Hal:** Go, hide thee behind the arras: the rest walk up above.
> Now, my masters, for a true face and good conscience.
> **Falstaff:** Both which I have had: but their date is out, and
> therefore I'll hide me. [*Hides behind the arras.*]
>
> act 2, scene 4, lines 478–90

When Sir John tells Hal he is at once a construct, a made-up man, yet also loyal despite his turning against his teacher, he gives the Prince his dare. Hal, who needs Falstaff to confess cowardice, hesitates at the edge of summoning the hangman. Falstaff denies Hal's premise, which is that all who flee are cowards and not realists. I thrill to Falstaff's defiance. He knows that a word from Hal hangs him. Even in this extremity, he jests wonderfully with a plague on his bringing up, meaning at once his nurture, his impending summoning to a trial, his mounting the steps to the gallows.

Each of us must decide why Hal chooses to defer the death of Sir John Falstaff. The Fat Knight falls asleep and snores behind the arras, scarcely evidence of terror. Hal is properly entertained when the snoring Falstaff is searched and his unpaid bill to Mistress Quickly reveals:

> **Hal:** O monstrous! but one half-penny-worth of bread to this intolerable deal of sack! What there is else, keep close; we'll read it at more advantage: there let him sleep till day. I'll to the court in the morning. We must all to the wars, and thy place shall be honourable. I'll procure this fat rogue a charge of foot; and I know his death will be a march of twelve-score.
>
> act 2, scene 4, lines 527–33

Hal's stance toward Falstaff is so ambiguous and so ambivalent that we may never grasp all of it. Here he is both amused and menacing. There are a multiplicity of Hals and a cosmological bevy of Falstaffs. I no longer scoff at anybody's Falstaff because my idolatry admits that even I behold a universe of Falstaffs, each of them persuasive and palpable.

CHAPTER 6

Bardolph's Nose

Sir John is at his glorious apogee in his exchange with Bardolph
in act 3, scene 3, beginning with a reference to the highway robbery on Gad's Hill in which he and his Boar's Head companions
set upon travelers with the Falstaffian cry: "They hate us youth."
Chased away by Hal and Poins in disguise, Falstaff strikes a blow
or two and then joins the other ruffians in dashing away.

> **Falstaff:** Bardolph, am I not fallen away vilely since this last
> action? Do I not bate? do I not dwindle? Why, my skin
> hangs about me like an old lady's loose gown; I am
> withered like an old apple-john. Well, I'll repent, and that
> suddenly, while I am in some liking; I shall be out of heart
> shortly, and then I shall have no strength to repent. And I
> have not forgotten what the inside of a church is made of,
> I am a peppercorn, a brewer's horse: the inside of a church!
> Company, villanous company, hath been the spoil of me.
> **Bardolph:** Sir John, you are so fretful you cannot live long.
>
> act 3, scene 3, 1–12

Poor Bardolph, always devoted and obtuse, warns the Fat
Knight that repentance is bad for his health:

> **Falstaff:** Why, there is it. Come sing me a bawdy song; make
> me merry. I was as virtuously given as a gentleman need

39

to be; virtuous enough; swore little; diced not above seven
times a week; went to a bawdy-house not above once in a
quarter—of an hour; paid money that I borrowed, three
of four times; lived well and in good compass: and now I
live out of all order, out of all compass.

Bardolph: Why, you are so fat, Sir John, that you must needs
be out of all compass, out of all reasonable compass, Sir
John.

Falstaff: Do thou amend thy face, and I'll amend my life: thou
art our admiral, thou bearest the lantern in the poop,
but 'tis in the nose of thee; thou art the Knight of the
Burning Lamp.

Bardolph: Why, Sir John, my face does you no harm.

act 3, scene 3, lines 13–28

Sir John exercises his laughing speech with an uneasy awareness
of sorrow to come. Bardolph, faithful and prosaic, urges the knight
to cast out anxiety. Falstaff's high humor returns as he commends
his sufficient virtue: to gamble only once a day, to seek out doxies
not more than every fifteen minutes, and to pay debts very occa-
sionally. I would not read "compass" here as moderation, since this
is Sir John Falstaff. He is himself the compass of all things. Bardolph's fiery nose and carbuncles inspire Falstaff to a Catherine
wheel of imagistic splendor. In turn they are a will-o'-the-wisp,
fireworks, bonfire, and most brilliantly a salamander:

Falstaff: No, I'll be sworn; I make as good use of it as many
a man doth of a Death's-head or a memento mori: I
never see thy face but I think upon hell-fire and Dives
that lived in purple; for there he is in his robes, burning,
burning. If thou wert any way given to virtue, I would
swear by thy face; my oath should be 'By this fire, that's

God's angel:' but thou art altogether given over; and
wert indeed, but for the light in thy face, the son of utter
darkness. When thou rannest up Gadshill in the night
to catch my horse, if I did not think thou hadst been an
ignis fatuus or a ball of wildfire, there's no purchase in
money. O, thou art a perpetual triumph, an everlasting
bonfire-light! Thou hast saved me a thousand marks
in links and torches, walking with thee in the night
betwixt tavern and tavern: but the sack that thou hast
drunk would have bought me lights as good cheap at
the dearest chandler's in Europe. I have maintained that
salamander of yours with fire any time this two and
thirty years; God reward me for it!

Bardolph: 'Sblood, I would my face were in your belly!

Falstaff: God-a-mercy! So should I be sure to be heart-
burned.

act 3, scene 3, lines 29–50

Embedded in Sir John's rhapsody is his first allusion to Luke
16: 19–26, a text everyone in the audience would have recognized:

There was a certain rich man, which was clothed in purple and
fine linen, and fared sumptuously every day:

And there was a certain beggar named Lazarus, which was
laid at his gate, full of sores,

And desiring to be fed with the crumbs which fell from the
rich man's table: moreover the dogs came and licked his sores.

And it came to pass, that the beggar died, and was carried by
the angels into Abraham's bosom: the rich man also died, and
was buried;

And in hell he lift up his eyes, being in torments, and seeth
Abraham afar off, and Lazarus in his bosom.

And he cried and said, Father Abraham, have mercy on me, and send Lazarus, that he may dip the tip of his finger in water, and cool my tongue; for I am tormented in this flame.

But Abraham said, Son, remember that thou in thy lifetime receivedst thy good things, and likewise Lazarus evil things: but now he is comforted, and thou art tormented.

And beside all this, between us and you there is a great gulf fixed: so that they which would pass from hence to you cannot; neither can they pass to us, that would come from thence.

Geneva Bible 1599

This severe parable of rejection haunts Falstaff. He will refer to it twice more and will enact it in the scene where the newly crowned Henry V banishes him. Mistress Quickly, describing the death of Falstaff in *Henry V*, transposes Abraham's bosom to Arthur's bosom, where she insists Sir John has found permanent haven.

In the Vulgate, St. Jerome's Latin version of the Bible, the certain rich man is a *dives*, hence Falstaff's vision of Dives, who lived in purple but now burns in hell. Shakespeare's audience, rejoicing in Falstaff, would have known that. James Joyce envied Shakespeare the playgoers at the Globe because they were more acutely aware than Joyce's readership of the possibilities of language. Shakespeare's trust was that he would be apprehended at several different levels. Falstaff's obsession with the parable of Dives and Lazarus is novelistic as well as dramatic. I find that my students respond with fascination when they study how intricately the five allusions and indirect references to the parable work through in the three plays.

Even the most acutely attuned of audiences in a theater has difficulty in fully apprehending the relation between the parable of Lazarus and Dives and the rejection of Falstaff by Hal. Reading a novel, say by Tolstoy or by Joyce, you can work out a pattern of allusions and deepening meanings by incessant rereadings. Shakespeare is as much the ancestor of the novel as he is of all drama after him.

The great gulf fixed is between Falstaff and Hal. I wince at the parable particularly when the dogs lick the leper's sores. Falstaff is a glutton and a freeloader but he is no Dives. He is generous, admittedly with what he has cadged, and there is no cruelty in him. I do not think that Sir John identifies himself either with rich man or with beggar. Rather he is tormented by the shape of the parable.

That shape is a vision of a purple-clad glutton refusing food and water to a starving leper. Dives rejects Lazarus and burns in hell. Far off he sees Lazarus resting in the bosom of father Abraham and he begs Abraham for the mercy of Lazarus dipping his finger in water and then cooling the tongue of the rich man tormented for eternity.

What is it to dread rejection? From the time when we were very young on through adolescence and maturity, we can fear inconsequence, ineptitude, the distress of abandonment. We fall in love impossibly as though defeat is our desire. Nothing in Falstaff's history suggests he ever married or suffered love for a woman beyond him. I am perplexed by his love for Hal. Is it for the son he never had? Or is it a teacher's pride and joy in his most gifted student?

I think back through my long life and remember the squalor of loneliness. As we age we worry about neglect. Falstaff is never alone on stage, unlike Hal. Bardolph and Nym, Pistol and Mistress Quickly, Doll Tearsheet and the boy who serves Falstaff are not other than motley and all lack wit. Are they the best Sir John could attract? The contrast to Hal returns us to the great gulf fixed between need and wavering patronage, as it was between Lazarus and Dives.

We have voyaged from Bardolph's nose to the damnation of Dives. Falstaff is more than aware how dark his odyssey will become. He senses as we do that there is no help for him. The sea of affliction will soak his heart through.

CHAPTER 7

Falstaff Rises in the Body

The battle of Shrewsbury between Hotspur's rebels and King Henry IV's loyalists was shrewdly envisioned by Orson Welles in his film *Chimes at Midnight* as a lethal mud bath. Our love of Falstaff is enhanced by his sly service in that messy imbroglio. He begins with his ragged recruits and cheerfully acknowledges his profit in exploiting Henry IV's draft of unwilling subjects:

> If I be not ashamed of my soldiers, I am a
> soused gurnet. I have misused the King's press
> damnably. I have got, in exchange of a hundred and
> fifty soldiers, three hundred and odd pounds. I press
> me none but good householders, yeomen's sons;
> inquire me out contracted bachelors, such as had been
> asked twice on the banns, such a commodity of warm
> slaves as had as lief hear the devil as a drum, such as
> fear the report of a caliver worse than a struck fowl or
> a hurt wild duck. I pressed me none but such toasts-
> and-butter, with hearts in their bellies no bigger than
> pins' heads, and they have bought out their services;
> and now my whole charge consists of ensigns,
> corporals, lieutenants, gentlemen of companies—slaves
> as ragged as Lazarus in the painted cloth, where the
> glutton's dogs licked his sores—and such as indeed
> were never soldiers, but discarded unjust servingmen,

younger sons to younger brothers, revolted tapsters and ostlers trade-fallen, the cankers of a calm world and a long peace, ten times more dishonourable ragged than an old feazed ensign. And such have I to fill up the rooms of them that have bought out their services that you would think that I had a hundred and fifty tattered prodigals lately come from swine-keeping, from eating draff and husks. A mad fellow met me on the way and told me I had unloaded all the gibbets and pressed the dead bodies. No eye hath seen such scarecrows. I'll not march through Coventry with them, that's flat. Nay, and the villains march wide betwixt the legs, as if they had gyves on; for indeed I had the most of them out of prison. There's but a shirt and a half in all my company, and the half shirt is two napkins tacked together and thrown over the shoulders like an herald's coat without sleeves; and the shirt, to say the truth, stolen from my host at Saint Albans, or the red-nose innkeeper of Daventry. But that's all one; they'll find linen enough on every hedge.

act 4, scene 2, lines 11–47

In this wonderful vaunt the shadow of Lazarus and Dives suddenly flickers: ". . . slaves as ragged as Lazarus in the painted cloth, where the glutton's dogs licked his sores . . ." The parable intrudes even unwanted. Falstaff is unaware that this vision of rejection haunts him. There are many instances of forlorn wretches scarcely clothed yet the harshest of all the sayings of Jesus will not let Falstaff alone.

Of course we condone Falstaff. Should your taste be for slaughter you may go elsewhere. Hal, for whom carnage is honorable, looks upon Falstaff's pariah conscripts with disapproval. Is Falstaff's reply heartless? "Tut, tut; good enough to toss; food for powder, food for powder; they'll fill a pit as well as better: tush, man, mortal men, mortal men." The issue is between power-mongers and realists. Is Falstaff mistaken? As a realist he is neither a coward nor callous. He knows that his unfortunate conscripts will die or be maimed only to keep Henry IV and Hal in power.

Recall that Sir John is past seventy in age. Not exactly in fighting condition, he nevertheless will *lead* his scarecrows into the midst of the battle:

> Though I could 'scape shot-free at London, I fear the shot here. Here's no scoring but upon the pate. Soft, who are you? Sir Walter Blunt. There's honour for you. Here's no vanity. I am as hot as molten lead and as heavy too. God keep lead out of me; I need no more weight than mine own bowels. I have led my ragamuffins where they are peppered; there's not three of my hundred and fifty left alive, and they are for the town's end, to beg during life.
>
> act 5, scene 3, lines 30–38

I have been chided for sentimentality when I observe Falstaff betrays and harms no one. Is Falstaff to blame for costing innocent men their lives? By that test we should more than blame King Henry IV and Hal for authentic brutality, sending so many to war. But blame is irrelevant. Do not moralize. Enjoy a passage in which Ralph Richardson triumphed:

> **Hal:** What, stand'st thou idle here? Lend me thy sword.
> Many a noble man lies stark and stiff
> Under the hoofs of vaunting enemies,
> Whose deaths are yet unrevenged. I prithee,
> Lend me thy sword.

Falstaff: O Hal, I prithee, give me leave to breathe awhile.
 Turk Gregory never did such deeds in arms as I have
 done this day. I have paid Percy, I have made him sure.
Hal: He is, indeed; and living to kill thee. I prithee, lend me
 thy sword.
Falstaff: Nay, before God, Hal, if Percy be alive, thou get'st not
 my sword; but take my pistol, if thou wilt.
Hal: Give it to me: what, is it in the case?
Falstaff: Ay, Hal; 'tis hot, 'tis hot; there's that will sack a city.
[Hal draws it out, and finds it to be a bottle of sack.]
Hal: What, is it a time to jest and dally now?
[He throws the bottle at him. Exit.]
Falstaff: Well, if Percy be alive, I'll pierce him. If he do come
 in my way, so: if he do not, if I come in his willingly, let
 him make a carbonado of me. I like not such grinning
 honour as Sir Walter hath: give me life: which if I can
 save, so; if not, honour comes unlooked for, and there's
 an end.

act 5, scene 3, lines 40–62

Shall we praise Shakespeare or Falstaff? Can they be separated? Sir John as an officer goes into battle with sword and pistol. So disdainful is he of the muck and butchery that he replaces the firearm with sack. Ralph Richardson danced nimbly aside dodging the thrown oloroso. It is a time to jest and dally in contempt of the bloodbath. Who would wish to quarrel with "give me life"?

Evidently, Hal would. Having slain Hotspur, he spies Falstaff playing dead:

Hal: What, old acquaintance! Could not all this flesh
Keep in a little life? Poor Jack, farewell!
I could have better spared a better man.

O, I should have a heavy miss of thee
If I were much in love with vanity!
Death hath not struck so fat a deer today,
Though many dearer, in this bloody fray.
Embowelled will I see thee by and by;
Till then, in blood by noble Percy lie.
[*Exit.*]

That is not exactly an expression of sorrow. Rather, it exudes relief. Falstaff is an inconvenient old acquaintance who will not have to be hanged. The slain Hotspur was noble while the apparently perished Fat Knight personified vanity. Neither we nor Falstaff are much moved by the promise of a dignified embowelling:

[*Falstaff riseth up.*]
Falstaff: Embowelled! If thou embowel me today, I'll give you
    leave to powder me, and eat me too, tomorrow. 'Sblood,
    'twas time to counterfeit, or that hot termagant Scot
    had paid me, scot and lot too. Counterfeit? I lie; I am
    no counterfeit. To die is to be a counterfeit, for he is but
    the counterfeit of a man who hath not the life of a man.
    But to counterfeit dying when a man thereby liveth is
    to be no counterfeit but the true and perfect image of
    life indeed. The better part of valour is discretion, in the
    which better part I have saved my life. 'Zounds, I am
    afraid of this gunpowder Percy, though he be dead. How
    if he should counterfeit too and rise? By my faith, I am
    afraid he would prove the better counterfeit. Therefore
    I'll make him sure, yea, and I'll swear I killed him. Why
    may not he rise as well as I? Nothing confutes me but
    eyes, and nobody sees me. Therefore, sirrah [*stabbing*

him], with a new wound in your thigh, come you along
with me.

act 5, scene 4, lines 101–28

The gulf between Hal and Falstaff widens to an abyss. The
Prince's reaction to the supposed death of his old companion is
dreadful. Hal returns to his obsession with vanity and promises
what was Falstaff an honorable embalming. In the Old Vic production, Ralph Richardson bounded up like a rubber ball with a
great cry of "emboweled?" The true piece of gold shrugs off Hal
the counterfeit and embraces the true and perfect image of life. A
beloved student who died at twenty-two in a car crash had given
me a mug with the inscription: "The better part of valor is discretion." Mourning her I never use the mug myself but am cheered
when my current students drink tea from it.

When Hal beholds the resurrected Falstaff he wonders if this is
a fantasy: "Thou art not what thou seem'st." Falstaff's grand rejoinder is "I am not a double man," as Hal clearly is. If there can be
a secular Resurrection, it would be Falstaff rising from the dead.
The spirit that surges in all of us, even in the face of death, mounts
to more life in the presence of the grandest personality in all of
Shakespeare.

CHAPTER 8

Foregrounding Falstaff

The passage from *Henry IV, Part 1* to *Part 2* is an appropriate crossing to foreground Falstaff. By "foregrounding" I mean "implying." What can we surmise about the development of personalities before the play opens?

Shakespeare implies a long foreground for the relationship between Hal and Falstaff. Inference here has to become a kind of speculation. When we first see them on stage together we are startled at the Prince's harshness and aggressivity. Falstaff evades the hostility but the foreboding of rejection is always there.

We do not know how far back the association between the usurper's son and the Fat Knight began. Clearly a prior warmth of good fellowship has drifted toward evanescence. Can we infer how so unlikely a friendship commenced?

It is not until Hal becomes monarch that his dormant shame at being the son of a usurping regicide is fully expressed. It would seem he sought out Falstaff as an act of truancy. Yet so brilliantly complex is Hal's nature that speculation becomes labyrinthine.

The marvelous freedom of *Henry IV* depends on a redistribution outward of the aggression that in the Sonnets is so frequently turned inward on the poet. But it is striking that Shakespeare, in dealing for the first time with the transmission of heritage across tension between father and son, alters his sources to eliminate direct expressions of the Prince's hostile or defiant feelings toward his father.

Much depends on how willing we are to share the English mythology of Henry V as the hero-king who conquered France and became a model of political success. Ostensibly the Henriad exalts that mythology. But if you read the Falstaffiad against that grain, you can question the human cost of the metamorphosis by which Hal becomes King Henry V. I like to think that Shakespeare would have agreed that Falstaff was as good as bread and wine. Who would say that of Henry V?

In Shakespeare as in life no one is wholly free. Chastened as I am in my love for Falstaff, whose flaws are so palpable, is he not at his best a giant image of human freedom? Like Falstaff, the poet of the Sonnets accepts the role of scapegoat. The link between the poet of the Sonnets and Falstaff is subtle, as here in Sonnet 125:

> Were't aught to me I bore the canopy,
> With my extern the outward honouring,
> Or laid great bases for eternity,
> Which prove more short than waste or ruining?
> Have I not seen dwellers on form and favour
> Lose all, and more, by paying too much rent,
> For compound sweet forgoing simple savour,
> Pitiful thrivers, in their gazing spent?
> No, let me be obsequious in thy heart,
> And take thou my oblation, poor but free,
> Which is not mix'd with seconds, knows no art
> But mutual render, only me for thee.
> > Hence, thou suborn'd informer! a true soul
> > When most impeach'd stands least in thy control.

Did Shakespeare regard himself as one of the "Pitiful thrivers, in their gazing spent"? Falstaff was not given to sonnets but try the experiment of hearing him deliver these lines to Hal. It would be out of character for him to be obsequious or fawning but is he the bread and wine offered to Hal as oblation, a sacrifice in a secular Eucharist? We could then speak of the Passion of Sir John Falstaff. Does he also die for love?

Falstaff loves Hal and urgently needs to be loved in return. Hamlet loves no one, certainly not himself, and does not need or want love from anyone. Lear loves Cordelia and is revered and loved by everyone in the tragedy who is not a monster.

We never will know precisely what Shakespeare felt he had accomplished in creating Sir John Falstaff. But it is clear that Falstaff created Shakespeare's second career in the theater, when he became playwright as well as actor. Falstaff captivated the audience, solidified Shakespeare's place in the Lord Chamberlain's men, and from early 1597 on began to enrich him. Probably Richard Burbage played Hal and William Sly, Hotspur. Shakespeare himself possibly played King Henry IV and the lively comic actor Will Kemp may have triumphed as Falstaff.

The Fat Knight became the rage of London. Queen Elizabeth, the nobility, the merchant class, and the groundlings all were delighted by his wit. Doubtless gratified, Shakespeare went on to *Henry IV, Part 2* and initially planned a central role for Falstaff in *Henry V*. Wisely, he confined Sir John to a death scene related by Mistress Quickly and to a few remarks by the Welsh Captain Fluellen. Unfortunately, he also composed *The Merry Wives of Windsor*, a ghastly comedy that is an unacceptable travesty of Falstaff. Legend is that Queen Elizabeth asked to see Sir John in love; it seems that Shakespeare may have grimaced his way through obedience and self-parody.

Is the secret of Falstaff's comic exuberance his need to be loved? All audiences did when the plays were first performed, and many readers and playgoers love him now, a spontaneous response not to be put aside by high-concept directors and the undead among scholars and journalists. We love his language. It is true gold. With the creation of Falstaff, Shakespeare discovered there were no limits to his art.

Shakespeare's prose in *Henry IV, Part 1* is radically different from any he had written before. Sir John speaks only prose and it has a buoyancy and zest that are unfailing. Falstaff's style permeates all who are of his company including Hal.

Falstaff's prose contaminates even Dr. Samuel Johnson, whose rolling periods cascade with orotund harmony. Oscar Wilde has Lady Augusta Bracknell in *The Importance of Being Earnest*, who would have been shocked to encounter Sir John, echo him:

> **Lady Bracknell:** The line is immaterial. Mr. Worthing, I
> confess I feel somewhat bewildered by what you have
> just told me. To be born, or at any rate bred, in a hand-
> bag, whether it had handles or not, seems to me to
> display a contempt for the ordinary decencies of family
> life that reminds one of the worst excesses of the
> French Revolution. And I presume you know what that
> unfortunate movement led to? As for the particular
> locality in which the hand-bag was found, a cloak-
> room at a railway station might serve to conceal a social
> indiscretion—has probably, indeed, been used for that
> purpose before now—but it could hardly be regarded as
> an assured basis for a recognised position in good society.
> **Jack:** May I ask you then what you would advise me to do?
> I need hardly say I would do anything in the world to
> ensure Gwendolen's happiness.
> **Lady Bracknell:** I would strongly advise you, Mr. Worthing, to
> try and acquire some relations as soon as possible, and to

make a definite effort to produce at any rate one parent, of either sex, before the season is quite over.

Jack: Well, I don't see how I could possibly manage to do that. I can produce the hand-bag at any moment. It is in my dressing-room at home. I really think that should satisfy you, Lady Bracknell.

Lady Bracknell: Me, sir! What has it to do with me? You can hardly imagine that I and Lord Bracknell would dream of allowing our only daughter—a girl brought up with the utmost care—to marry into a cloak-room, and form an alliance with a parcel? Good morning, Mr. Worthing!

act 1, scene 1, lines 568–96

Falstaff would have disdained her sentiments but might have recognized his influence upon the formidable Augusta Bracknell. Hal is so immersed in Falstaff's language that when he teases poor Francis and then muses on his own vagaries he does so in the accent of Sir John: "I am now of all humours that have showed themselves humours since the old days of goodman Adam to the pupil age of this present twelve o'clock at midnight." The habit of biblical reference, another Falstaffian mode, is illuminated by the Epilogue to *Henry IV, Part 2*. An actor steps in front of the fallen curtain and addresses the audience directly:

One word more, I beseech you. If you be not too much cloyed with fat meat, our humble author will continue the story, with Sir John in it, and make you merry with fair Katharine of France; where, for anything I know, Falstaff shall die of a sweat, unless already a' be killed with your hard opinions; for Oldcastle died a martyr and this is not the man. My tongue is weary; when my legs are too, I will bid you good night.

Epilogue, lines 26–34

Shakespeare originally wished to call his Fat Knight Sir John Oldcastle but wisely desisted when Oldcastle's descendants objected. The historical Sir John Oldcastle was a close friend of King Henry V but then rebelled and was burned alive for heresy. He was a Lollard, the reform movement inaugurated by John Wycliffe, who translated the Bible and was a forerunner of English Protestantism. Instead Shakespeare went to the historical soldier Sir John Fastolf who was accused of abandoning John Talbot, the Earl of Shrewsbury, the great commander of the English army fighting against France during the Hundred Years' War. Fastolf was exonerated but Shakespeare appropriated his name for the Immortal Sir John Falstaff.

Though he parodies biblical texts incessantly, no one would call Falstaff a Lollard or a Puritan. Yet there is a curious strain of spiritual yearning in Sir John, haunted as he is by the terrible parable of Dives and Lazarus. Henry V describes himself as a Christian king yet he orders his prisoners to be killed and threatens to sack Harfleur:

> If not, why, in a moment look to see
> The blind and bloody soldier with foul hand
> Defile the locks of your shrill-shrieking daughters,
> Your fathers taken by the silver beards,
> And their most reverend heads dashed to the walls,
> Your naked infants spitted upon pikes,
> Whiles the mad mothers with their howls confused
> Do break the clouds, as did the wives of Jewry
> At Herod's bloody-hunting slaughtermen.
> What say you? will you yield, and this avoid?
> Or, guilty in defence, be thus destroyed?
>
> act 3, scene 3, lines 33–43

One wonders at Shakespeare's irony, or is it Hal's? The savage glee here is politic but surely Henry V realizes that as Christian monarch he would preside over a new Massacre of the Innocents. Gone for now is the language of Sir John Falstaff who lies dead in Eastcheap.

CHAPTER 9

Darkening Falstaff

Rereading *Henry IV, Part 2* is an experience joyous and somber. There is no lessening of Shakespeare's powers, but a kind of rancidity intrudes. A trait that Shakespeare later carries to limits in *Troilus and Cressida, All's Well That Ends Well,* and *Measure for Measure* attains a bulk that shadows Sir John Falstaff.

It is a commonplace that the gulf between Hal and Falstaff widens progressively in *Part 2*. We see them together only once before the final rejection. Each darkens in a way of his own until substance yields to shadow. Henry V is crowned as Sir John and his ragamuffins are ordered to the Fleet prison by the Lord Chief Justice.

Falstaff's Bad Angel, the Chief Justice cannot be deterred by Sir John's defiance. In the second scene of *Part 2* Falstaff's entrance is in the street, with his tiny Page staggering after him carrying the Fat Knight's sword and buckler:

> **Falstaff:** Sirrah, you giant, what says the doctor to my water?
> **Page:** He said, sir, the water itself was a good healthy water;
>   but, for the party that owed it, he might have more
>   diseases than he knew for.
> **Falstaff:** Men of all sorts take a pride to gird at me. The brain
>   of this foolish-compounded clay, man, is not able to
>   invent anything that intends to laughter, more than
>   I invent, or is invented on me; I am not only witty in

myself, but the cause that wit is in other men. I do here walk before thee like a sow that hath overwhelmed all her litter but one. If the Prince put thee into my service for any other reason than to set me off, why then I have no judgment. Thou whoreson mandrake, thou art fitter to be worn in my cap than to wait at my heels. I was never manned with an agate till now, but I will inset you, neither in gold nor silver, but in vile apparel, and send you back again to your master for a jewel,—the juvenal the Prince your master, whose chin is not yet fledged. I will sooner have a beard grow in the palm of my hand than he shall get one off his cheek; and yet he will not stick to say his face is a face-royal. God may finish it when He will, 'tis not a hair amiss yet. He may keep it still at a face-royal, for a barber shall never earn sixpence out of it. And yet he'll be crowing as if he had writ man ever since his father was a bachelor. He may keep his own grace, but he's almost out of mine, I can assure him. What said Master Dommelton about the satin for my short cloak and my slops?

Page: He said, sir, you should procure him better assurance than Bardolph: he would not take his bond and yours, he liked not the security.

Falstaff: Let him be damned like the glutton! Pray God his tongue be hotter! A whoreson Achitophel! A rascally yea-forsooth knave, to bear a gentleman in hand, and then stand upon security! The whoreson smooth-pates do now wear nothing but high shoes and bunches of keys at their girdles; and if a man is through with them in honest taking up, then they must stand upon security. I had as lief they would put ratsbane in my mouth as offer to stop it with security. I looked a' should have

sent me two and twenty yards of satin, as I am a true
knight, and he sends me 'security'! Well, he may sleep
in security; for he hath the horn of abundance, and the
lightness of his wife shines through it; and yet cannot
he see, though he have his own lanthorn to light him.
Where's Bardolph?

Page: He's gone into Smithfield to buy your worship a horse.

Falstaff: I bought him in Paul's, and he'll buy me a horse in
Smithfield. And I could get me but a wife in the stews, I
were manned, horsed, and wived.

act 1, scene 2, lines 1–54

This has all of Falstaff's ocean of language yet the beauty of
laughter wanes. Sir John speaks a true credo: "I am not only witty
in myself, but the cause that wit is in other men." Do we laugh
or flinch at the wonderful: "I do here walk before thee like a sow
that hath overwhelmed all her litter but one"? Increasingly Falstaff
acts out the role of himself. There is a cost to this confirmation.
The great improviser seems more studied, given over to unbridled
extravagance. With this a new tone of ridicule is turned against
Hal. Beneath the savage comedy the old uneasiness courses on.
The sensible tailor becomes Dives the glutton, his tongue hot in
hell, and also Achitophel who betrayed King David for Absalom
the rebellious son.

The entrance of the Lord Chief Justice provokes Falstaff to bel-
ligerent defiance of the law and to a hyperbolic assertion of youth
against age. In *Part 1* Sir John led the foray of highwaymen with
the grand cry: "They hate us young!" Here the struggle against time
coalesces with the contest against death, the final form of change.

Lord Chief Justice: Do you set down your name in the
scroll of youth, that are written down old with all the

61

characters of age? Have you not a moist eye, a dry
hand, a yellow cheek, a white beard, a decreasing leg,
an increasing belly? Is not your voice broken, your wind
short, your chin double, your wit single, and every part
about you blasted with antiquity? And will you yet call
yourself young? Fie, fie, fie, Sir John!

Falstaff: My lord, I was born about three of the clock in the
afternoon, with a white head, and something a round
belly. For my voice, I have lost it with hallooing, and
singing of anthems. To approve my youth further, I
will not; the truth is, I am only old in judgment and
understanding; and he that will caper with me for a
thousand marks, let him lend me the money, and have at
him! For the box of the ear that the Prince gave you, he
gave it like a rude prince, and you took it like a sensible
lord. I have checked him for it; and the young lion
repents—[*aside*] marry, not in ashes and sackcloth, but in
new silk and old sack.

act 1, scene 2, lines 177–98

At eighty-six I have a moist eye, a dry hand, a yellow cheek, a
white beard if I let it grow, a greatly decreasing leg, but not much
belly any longer. Most certainly my voice is broken, my wind
very short, and on a bad day like this I feel blasted with antiquity.
Though Falstaff darkens he charms forever with: "My lord, I was
born about three of the clock in the afternoon, with a white head,
and something a round belly." His cognitive strength is enormous
and still undervalued but his judgment is always questionable.
Going on three-quarters of a century he resolutely remains a child.

As act 2 of *Henry IV, Part 2* opens, Mistress Quickly enters with
Fang and Snare to arrest Sir John for his vast unpaid debt to her,
Hostess of the Boar's Head Tavern. Her incessant use of the wrong

word with a similar sound is the ancestress of Mrs. Malaprop in Richard Brinsley Sheridan's 1775 comedy *The Rivals*. In 1966 my wife and I saw a splendid production directed by Glen Byam Shaw at the Haymarket in London. Ralph Richardson astonished as Sir Joseph Surface and Margaret Rutherford alas was losing her memory yet still delighted. Just the year before, in 1965, Orson Welles directed *Chimes at Midnight*, though it was not released until later. Margaret Rutherford was at her best as Mistress Quickly. When I read and teach *Henry IV* she is the image in my mind as intensely as Richardson is Falstaff:

> Snare: It may chance cost some of our lives, for he will stab.
> Mistress Quickly: Alas the day, take heed of him—he stabbed me in mine own house, most beastly in good faith. A cares not what mischief he does, if his weapon be out; he will foin like any devil; he will spare neither man, woman, nor child.
> Fang: If I can close with him, I care not for his thrust.
> Mistress Quickly: No, nor I neither; I'll be at your elbow.
> Fang: And I but fist him once, an a' come but within my vice,—
> Mistress Quickly: I am undone by his going, I warrant you, he's an infinitive thing upon my score. Good Master Fang, hold him sure; good Master Snare, let him not 'scape. A' comes continuantly to Pie Corner—saving your manhoods—to buy a saddle, and he is indited to dinner to the Lubber's Head in Lumbert Street, to Master Smooth's the silkman. I pray you, since my exion is entered, and my case so openly known to the world, let him be brought in to his answer. A hundred mark is a long one for a poor lone woman to bear, and I have borne, and borne, and borne, and have been fubbed off, and fubbed off, and fubbed off, from this day to that day,

that it is a shame to be thought on. There is no honesty
in such dealing, unless a woman should be made an ass,
and a beast, to bear every knave's wrong.

act 2, scene 1, lines 11–37

The sexual play on stabbing with a weapon, reinforced by "foin,"
a fencing thrust, is common enough but Shakespeare vivifies it by
the agency of Falstaff. Hostess Quickly is contaminated, like so
many others, by Falstaff's language though she cannot manage it
with the malapropism of "infinitive" for infinite.

[*Enter Sir John Falstaff, Bardolph, and Page.*]

Mistress Quickly: Yonder he comes, and that arrant malmsey-
nose knave Bardolph with him. Do your offices, do your
offices, Master Fang and Master Snare, do me, do me, do
me your offices.

Falstaff: How now! whose mare's dead? What's the matter?

Fang: Sir John, I arrest you at the suit of Mistress Quickly.

Falstaff: Away, varlets! Draw, Bardolph! Cut me off the
villain's head! Throw the quean in the channel!

Mistress Quickly: Throw me in the channel? I'll throw thee in
the channel. Wilt thou, wilt thou, thou bastardly rogue?
Murder! Murder! Ah, thou honeysuckle villain, wilt thou
kill God's officers and King's? Ah, thou honeyseed rogue!
thou art a honey-seed; a man-queller and a woman-
queller.

Falstaff: Keep them off, Bardolph.

Fang: A rescue! a rescue!

Mistress Quickly: Good people, bring a rescue or two. Thou
wo't, wo't thou wo't, wo't ta? Do, do, thou rogue! do, thou
hemp-seed!

Page: Away, you scullion! you rampallian! you fustilarian! I'll
tickle your catastrophe.

act 2, scene 1, lines 38–59

The Page, Sir John's pupil, castigates Quickly as a rampallian or
ruffian, and as a frowsy plump woman. Threatening to spank the
spunky Hostess, the tiny boy improbably warns her he will "tickle
your catastrophe"!

The Lord Chief Justice enters, intervenes, and Falstaff pretends
to yield:

Falstaff: What is the gross sum that I owe thee?

Mistress Quickly: Marry, if thou wert an honest man, thyself
and the money too. Thou didst swear to me upon a parcel-
gilt goblet, sitting in my Dolphin chamber, at the round
table, by a sea-coal fire, upon Wednesday in Wheeson
week, when the Prince broke thy head for liking his
father to a singing-man of Windsor—thou didst swear
to me then, as I was washing thy wound, to marry me,
and make me my lady thy wife. Canst thou deny it? Did
not goodwife Keech the butcher's wife come in then
and call me gossip Quickly?—coming in to borrow a
mess of vinegar, telling us she had a good dish of prawns,
whereby thou didst desire to eat some, whereby I told
thee they were ill for green wound? And didst thou not,
when she was gone down stairs, desire me to be no more
so familiarity with such poor people, saying that ere long
they should call me madam? And didst thou not kiss me,
and bid me fetch thee thirty shillings? I put thee now to
thy book oath, deny it if thou canst.

act 2, scene 1, lines 82–101

This is Quickly at her most winsome, perpetually beguiled by the scamp Falstaff, and yet a wholesome spirit who appeals both to our laughter and to our sympathy. Artist of dissembling, the great Falstaff meets the occasion with fresh effrontery:

Falstaff: My lord, this is a poor mad soul, and she says up and down the town that her eldest son is like you. She hath been in good case, and the truth is, poverty hath distracted her. But for these foolish officers, I beseech you I may have redress against them.

Lord Chief Justice: Sir John, Sir John, I am well acquainted with your manner of wrenching the true cause the false way. It is not a confident brow, nor the throng of words that come with such more than impudent sauciness from you, can thrust me from a level consideration. You have, as it appears to me, practised upon the easy yielding spirit of this woman, and made her serve your uses both in purse and in person.

Mistress Quickly: Yea, in truth, my lord.

Lord Chief Justice: Pray thee, peace. Pay her the debt you owe her, and unpay the villainy you have done with her; the one you may do with sterling money, and the other with current repentance.

Falstaff: My lord, I will not undergo this sneap without reply. You call honourable boldness impudent sauciness; if a man will make curtsy and say nothing, he is virtuous. No, my lord, my humble duty remembered, I will not be your suitor. I say to you I do desire deliverance from these officers, being upon hasty employment in the King's affairs.

Lord Chief Justice: You speak as having power to do wrong;

but answer in the effect of your reputation, and satisfy
the poor woman.

Falstaff: Come hither, hostess.

act 2, scene 1, lines 102–31

As always, we enjoy Sir John's outrageousness, though it is
poignant, even a little heartbreaking, to hear Mistress Quickly
again suborned. She will tend him when he is dying, little indeed
as he merits it. Falstaff heaps affront upon ire: "My lord, this
is a poor mad soul, and she says up and down the town that
her eldest son is like you." And Quickly succumbs again all too
quickly:

Mistress Quickly: Well, you shall have it, though I pawn my
gown. I hope you'll come to supper. You'll pay me all
together?

Falstaff: Will I live? [*to Bardolph*] Go, with her, with her!
Hook on, hook on!

Mistress Quickly: Will you have Doll Tearsheet meet you at
supper?

Falstaff: No more words, let's have her.

act 2, scene 1, lines 156–62

This is Falstaff darkening but he was never one of the sons of
light; his hidden anguish is concealed by wit. No, sons of light are
not to be found in the *Henry IV* plays, and why should we want
them anyway? Shakespeare's wisdom rivals and overgoes the moral
philosophers and the classical theologians. Ludwig Wittgenstein
ambivalently regarded Shakespeare as having been primarily a creator of language. Falstaff, of all Shakespeare's personalities, is a
creator of language. Falstaff is a prime instance of how meaning

is engendered rather than repeated. Falstaff is excess, overthrow, extravagance—the prodigal of dissipation.

I term Sir John the Sage of Eastcheap. Wisdom is where you can find it. What does Falstaff teach? Like Shakespeare, he does not teach: he insinuates; he surrounds and contains us; he beckons and disturbs. Darkening, he darkens us. And so he threatens the very vitality he has given us as his greatest gift.

CHAPTER 10

Shakespeare Darkening

I find it fortunate we know so little about Shakespeare's inward life. Reading the plays and the Sonnets you could believe he was indeed everyone and no one, as Jorge Luis Borges observed. He composes as though he knew everything and nothing. It is idle to wonder whether he was Catholic or Protestant, bisexual or not, happily married or estranged, humanist or nihilist. He contains everything and everyone. We cannot usefully study him from the outside because we are Jonahs inside the whale.

Many readers and playgoers experience a sense that certain of Shakespeare's personalities relate intimately to his concealed inwardness. Falstaff and Hamlet impress me as being creations nearest to his center or centers. Since Shakespeare's circumference is cosmic and ultimately beyond our ken, he seems to vacillate from center to center. Like certain conceptions of God his center is nowhere.

Though Shakespeare owed much to his precursors—Ovid, Chaucer, the Geneva Bible, Christopher Marlowe—what mattered most was his influence upon himself. Where in the prior plays can we discover the ancestry of Falstaff?

Perhaps there are touches both of Bottom and of Puck in Sir John yet I hear more originating traces of Falstaff's brio and soaring language in the Bastard Faulconbridge, the wonderful invention Shakespeare inserts into *King John*, written the year before the Henry IV plays. The illegitimate son of Richard the Lion-

69

heart, Faulconbridge trades his inheritance for the title Sir Richard Plantagenet and becomes the leader of the forces of King John, Lionheart's younger brother, and Eleanor of Aquitaine, mother of Lionheart and John and so the Bastard's grandmother. Something new enters Shakespeare when the Bastard soliloquizes:

A foot of honour better than I was,
But many a many foot of land the worse.
Well, now can I make any Joan a lady.
'Good den, Sir Richard!'—'God-a-mercy, fellow!'—
And if his name be George, I'll call him Peter;
For new-made honour doth forget men's names:
'Tis too respective and too sociable
For your conversion. Now your traveller,
He and his toothpick at my worship's mess,
And when my knightly stomach is suffic'd,
Why then I suck my teeth and catechise
My picked man of countries: 'My dear sir,'
Thus, leaning on mine elbow, I begin,
'I shall beseech you'—that is question now;
And then comes answer like an Absey book:
'O sir,' says answer, 'at your best command;
At your employment; at your service, sir;'
'No, sir,' says question, 'I, sweet sir, at yours:'
And so, ere answer knows what question would,
Saving in dialogue of compliment,
And talking of the Alps and Apennines,
The Pyrenean and the river Po,
It draws toward supper in conclusion so.
But this is worshipful society,
And fits the mounting spirit like myself,
For he is but a bastard to the time

That doth not smack of observation;
And so am I, whether I smack or no;
And not alone in habit and device,
Exterior form, outward accoutrement,
But from the inward motion to deliver
Sweet, sweet, sweet poison for the age's tooth:
Which, though I will not practise to deceive,
Yet, to avoid deceit, I mean to learn;
For it shall strew the footsteps of my rising.

act 1, scene 1, lines 182–216

The Bastard mocks societal politeness and then mounts up to what might be Shakespeare's credo: "But from the inward motion to deliver / Sweet, sweet, sweet poison for the age's tooth." The sweet poison of flattery emanates from the inward motion of a poetic mind to heal an era's spiritual toothache. That motion is a violence from within that cannot hope to diminish killing and royal rivalries. But it helps to give us a new kind of Shakespearean personality in the Bastard, one who presages Falstaff. Here is the Bastard soliloquizing in reaction to the mutual betrayal by the Kings of England and France of their supposed moral purpose:

Mad world! mad kings! mad composition!
John, to stop Arthur's title in the whole,
Hath willingly departed with a part,
And France, whose armour conscience buckled on,
Whom zeal and charity brought to the field
As God's own soldier, rounded in the ear
With that same purpose-changer, that sly devil,
That broker, that still breaks the pate of faith,
That daily break-vow, he that wins of all,
Of kings, of beggars, old men, young men, maids,

Who, having no external thing to lose
But the word 'maid,' cheats the poor maid of that,
That smooth-faced gentleman, tickling Commodity,
Commodity, the bias of the world,
The world, who of itself is peised well,
Made to run even upon even ground,
Till this advantage, this vile-drawing bias,
This sway of motion, this Commodity,
Makes it take head from all indifferency,
From all direction, purpose, course, intent:

act 2, scene 1, lines 561–80

"Commodity" here is more than selfish gain. It is a kind of god, a Mammon whose service excludes the true God. In our world of corrupt bankers and rapacious brokers and hedge-fund varlets, commodity means pretty much what Shakespeare, through this eloquent Bastard, calls it: a shameless whoremongery that defrauds so many of us.

And this same bias, this commodity,
This bawd, this broker, this all-changing word,
Clapp'd on the outward eye of fickle France,
Hath drawn him from his own determined aid,
From a resolved and honourable war,
To a most base and vile-concluded peace.
And why rail I on this commodity?
But for because he hath not woo'd me yet:
Not that I have the power to clutch my hand,
When his fair angels would salute my palm;
But for my hand, as unattempted yet,
Like a poor beggar, raileth on the rich.
Well, whiles I am a beggar, I will rail

And say there is no sin but to be rich;
And being rich, my virtue then shall be
To say there is no vice but beggary.
Since kings break faith upon commodity,
Gain, be my lord, for I will worship thee!

act 2, scene 1, lines 581–98

The Bastard is not outraged but enjoys his own language of denunciation. He does not mean what he says, but never worships gain. Fighting to save England and his uncle King John, he will serve the survivors after John's death. In his accent I hear an inverse prelude to Falstaff's sly hunger for commodity. Like Falstaff, who glories in language, the Bastard intoxicates us. He is a truth-teller as Falstaff is, except when the Fat Knight sees an advantage in lying. Neither personality worships commodity, though the perpetually out-of-pocket Falstaff cadges whatever he can.

Shylock also precedes Falstaff in Shakespeare's career, again by a year. Kenneth Gross in his *Shylock Is Shakespeare* (2006) meditates upon the lower depths of Shylock's enigmatic relation to Shakespeare the dramatist. I cannot hold Shylock and Falstaff in my mind at once. Each personality is pungent beyond pungency. Have they anything in common? Shylock has a persecution mania and is tormented by hatred, as much within him as without. Falstaff wants and needs the audience's love, and fears the rejection that is at Shylock's core. Shylock is not acting the part of Shylock. He carries the curse of his people, and of his own joyless existence. And yet, like Falstaff, he holds the stage and renders the other characters into so many shadows. Even Shakespeare is not wholly capable of making Portia a mighty opposite for Shylock to confront. Nor can Hal be the center of the *Henry IV* plays despite Shakespeare's prodigious powers. Falstaff increasingly saddens me as I grow older. Since he is life itself and vitality must wane, I mourn for him in a way not wholly different from my sorrowing for dying and dead friends.

Forerunners among Shakespeare's personalities do not presage the largeness of Sir John Falstaff. After him will come Hamlet and then Iago, Lear, Macbeth, and Cleopatra, all of them Falstaff's true peers in Shakespearean drama. I recall that the admirable Irish novelist John Banville once chided me gently for contending that Shakespeare was cognitively more acute even than David Hume or Ludwig Wittgenstein. Banville rightly said that Shakespeare practiced a Wittgensteinian *showing*. I now agree with Banville though I still cannot discover the limits of Shakespeare's thinking.

If one is not Dr. Samuel Johnson, there are incapacities one cannot surmount. Johnson praised Shakespeare for rendering an expanded consciousness agreeable to us. I follow in Johnson's wake. It has never been clear to me how a teacher and critic of Shakespeare can avoid engulfment by him. More crucially, this predicament has engrossed all post-Shakespearean dramatists, poets, and novelists. Tolstoy deplored Shakespeare yet could not escape him. His wonderful late short novel *Hadji Murad* is Shakespearean in its vivid personalities and a fascinating detachment.

The Tragedy of Hamlet, Prince of Denmark haunts modern drama from Goethe on to Ibsen, Chekhov, Shaw, Pirandello, Brecht, Beckett, and Stoppard. The novels of Stendhal, Balzac, Victor Hugo, Flaubert, and Proust all absorb Shakespeare, as do those of Dostoevsky and Turgenev. In English, the catalog is vast and includes Samuel Richardson, Henry Fielding, Sir Walter Scott, Charles Dickens, George Eliot, the Brontës, George Meredith, and, overwhelmingly, James Joyce's *Ulysses*. American literature is obsessed by Shakespeare: Herman Melville, Emily Dickinson, Mark Twain, Henry James, Wallace Stevens, Ernest Hemingway, William Faulkner.

English poets from John Milton on to William Blake, William

Wordsworth, Samuel Taylor Coleridge, Byron, Shelley, Keats all write in Shakespeare's shadow. That shadow is an inspiration but nothing is got for nothing and Shakespeare is also an inhibition.

I return to Shakespeare's own darkening as he moves from Shylock through Falstaff to Hamlet, Iago, Lear, Macbeth, Cleopatra. Can we speak of Shakespeare's personality? Some of his contemporaries called him "gentle" and the few shreds of preserved gossip suggest he was amiable and modest. He contrasts to his friend Ben Jonson's burly assertiveness and to Christopher Marlowe's violent nature. Nothing of his personality is revealed in most of the plays or the Sonnets. And yet I intuit something deeply personal in his creation of Falstaff and Hamlet. Still, our surmises are defeated because we lack information. Instead there is the subtle movement from play to play, character to character.

In a fifteen-year span, 1596–1611, Shylock, Falstaff, Hamlet, Iago, Lear, Macbeth, Cleopatra, Prospero came into being. With them came Juliet, Rosalind, Malvolio, Leontes, a myriad of others. *King Lear* alone is crowded by Edmund, Edgar, Cordelia, and the Fool in addition to the great King. It seems incredible that one poet-dramatist accomplished that universe of personalities. Shakespeare's actions have become our emotions. His dreams people our thoughts. In fourteen consecutive months he composed *King Lear*, revised it, went on to *Macbeth* and without a break opened the vast vistas of *Antony and Cleopatra*. Even he may have suffered, if not exhaustion, a sea change in which there was a withdrawal from passion to a kind of quietism. From *Coriolanus* on to *The Winter's Tale* and *The Tempest*, a new kind of sorrow arrives.

After *The Tempest*, Shakespeare collaborated with John Fletcher on *The Two Noble Kinsmen* and perhaps on *Henry VIII*. There appears to be a lost play, *Cardenio*, written by Fletcher and Shakespeare. That takes us to 1613; Shakespeare died May 3, 1616, soon after his fifty-second birthday. We do not know what killed him.

There is an increasing preoccupation with venereal disease in *Measure for Measure*, *Troilus and Cressida*, *Timon of Athens*, and in the closing Sonnets. The treatment for syphilis included ample dosing with mercury. Did that hasten Shakespeare's demise?

In the Shakespearean contribution to *The Two Noble Kinsmen* there are traces of a violent turn against the male sexual drive. Anthony Burgess and I had several good-natured disagreements as to why Shakespeare wrote nothing in the last two and a half years of his life. Anthony insisted that syphilis had deprived the greatest of poets of any desire to imagine fresh personalities. I was skeptical and the matter still seems to me incapable of resolution. Mercury poisoning is very dreadful but we just do not know if that was involved.

Falstaff, only when dying, abandons the affirmation of human sexuality. He is the mortal god of our vitalism and of our capacity for joyous play of every kind.

I remain inclined to believe that Shakespeare, like his Hamlet, chose the rest of silence. Shakespeare, particularly in *King Lear*, raised the vision of human suffering to an apotheosis. Remorse for trespass is a darkening in most of us. The most capacious of souls may have recoiled from his own representation of suffering and its costs for us and to himself. If indeed Falstaff usurped Shakespeare's crown of vivacity, that remains the perpetual glory of the insouciant wit who presides over us all.

CHAPTER 11

Who Plays the King

There are scholars who contend that the Henriad begins with *The Tragedy of King Richard the Second*. Walter Pater, the great Aesthetic Critic, remarked that Richard was "an exquisite poet." As Shakespeare rendered him, Richard II was a better Metaphysical Poet than he was a king. Richard's personality is victimized by his own language. We all know friends or acquaintances who have a propensity for augmenting their catastrophes by excessive lamentations. Shakespeare's *Richard II* has a genius for enhancing misfortune:

> For God's sake, let us sit upon the ground
> And tell sad stories of the death of kings;
> How some have been deposed; some slain in war,
> Some haunted by the ghosts they have deposed;
> Some poison'd by their wives: some sleeping kill'd;
> All murder'd: for within the hollow crown
> That rounds the mortal temples of a king
> Keeps Death his court and there the antic sits,
> Scoffing his state and grinning at his pomp,
> Allowing him a breath, a little scene,
> To monarchize, be fear'd and kill with looks,
> Infusing him with self and vain conceit,
> As if this flesh which walls about our life,
> Were brass impregnable, and humour'd thus

Comes at the last and with a little pin
Bores through his castle wall, and farewell king!
Cover your heads and mock not flesh and blood
With solemn reverence: throw away respect,
Tradition, form and ceremonious duty,
For you have but mistook me all this while:
I live with bread like you, feel want,
Taste grief, need friends: subjected thus,
How can you say to me, I am a king?

act 3, scene 2, lines 155–77

The sad story of Richard II's death is altered by Shakespeare from the obscure historical record that holds that the deposed monarch was starved to death by Henry IV. In Shakespeare he is murdered by order of his usurper, who then feebly disowns the regicide. This central premise of the Henriad is handled with deft artistry. Henry IV, from start to finish, is bedeviled by rebellions against his barely legitimate authority. Guilt-stricken, he longs to expiate by leading a crusade to recover Jerusalem, an absurdly unlikely possibility.

Everyone in the Henriad, except for Hotspur and the other rebels, is in thrall to him. He cannot absorb us as Falstaff does and yet he holds his own on stage with the Fat Knight, which is extraordinary.

The two parts of *Henry IV*, taken together, show us Shakespeare at his most generous. Only *Hamlet* and *King Lear* are this large. All interpretations of *Hamlet* are questionable, and *The Tragedy of King Lear* is beyond our apprehension. *Henry IV* alternates between contrary worlds, and Hal is the matrix that gives form to the whirligig embracing King Henry IV and Hotspur at one pole and Falstaff at the other. Except for Hotspur, who dies at the close of *Part 1*, the quarrels of the court and the rebels pale when Falstaff commands the stage.

Take Falstaff out of the plays and you get the empty sensation I experience when moving from *Henry IV* to *Henry V*. And yet how can you account for the simultaneity of a stage that holds King Henry IV and Sir John Falstaff? They belong to different orders of being. Henry IV is careworn and inwardly consumed by agenbite of inwit. Falstaff thrusts cares away and would regard remorse as a dark idolatry alien to his vital self. The parable of Dives and Lazarus shadows Sir John but he evades it until, at the close of *Part 2*, he rushes toward it as though seeking an end to forebodings. Does he reject himself before Hal does?

In *Wuthering Heights*, Catherine Earnshaw is the troubled forge caught between the antithetical realms of Heathcliff and Edgar Linton. Emily Brontë's rare achievement is to bring together a visionary and a more mundane perspective that collide in the heroine and at last must destroy her. Shakespeare, vast beyond belief, juxtaposes Falstaff who is natural-all-too-natural with historical figures who become insubstantial in his presence.

Why did the Prince first seek out Falstaff? It is insufficient to argue that he was in flight from his father's crimes of usurpation and regicide. W. H. Auden, in his essay "The Prince's Dog," suggestively indicated the initial surprise when Sir John and his riff-raff show us Hal's descent into dissipation:

At a performance, my immediate reaction is to wonder what Falstaff is doing in this play at all. At the end of *Richard II*, we were told that the Heir Apparent has taken up with a dissolute crew of "unrestrained loose companions." What sort of bad company would one expect to find Prince Hal keeping when the curtain rises on *Henry IV*? Surely, one could expect to see him surrounded by daring, rather sinister juvenile delinquents and beautiful gold-digging whores. But whom do we meet in the Boar's Head? A fat, cowardly tosspot, old enough to be his father, two down-at-heel hangers-on, a slatternly hostess and only one whore, who is not in her earliest youth either; all of them seedy, and, by any worldly standards, including those of the criminal classes, all of them *failures*. Surely, one thinks, an Heir Apparent, sowing his wild oats, could have picked himself a more exciting crew than that.

What Auden omits is not so much the wit and counter-wisdom of Sir John but the surging bloom and bounce of his intellect. Falstaff loves his own language and teaches Hal the idiomatic skills that give King Henry V an eloquence founded on the common tongue. The myth of Henry V is that England never had a true king before him. I am not a historian or a theater critic and wonder in what sense Hal/Henry V is "true." From a Falstaffian perspective, Hal is a counterfeit and so is Henry IV. They are fraudulent.

Throughout *The Chronicle History of Henry V*, the triumphant King displays an eloquence to match all occasions and to beguile all men. His supple command may have a root in Falstaff's spell cast over the audience, yet that seems simplistic. Hal's considerable gifts for high good humor and for a lively sense of otherness are native to him. One wonders that he is the son of Henry IV, who nevertheless has a shrewd awareness of Hal's nature:

> For he is gracious if he be observ'd,
> He hath a tear for pity, and a hand
> Open as day for melting charity;
> Yet notwithstanding, being incens'd, he's flint,
> As humorous as winter, and as sudden
> As flaws congealed in the spring of day.
> His temper, therefore, must be well observ'd.
> Chide him for faults, and do it reverently,

When you perceive his blood inclin'd to mirth;
But, being moody, give him time and scope,
Till that his passions, like a whale on ground,
Confound themselves with working.

Henry IV, Part 2, act 4, scene 4, lines 30–41

Shakespeare chides no one and teaches us to emulate him. I therefore recant some of my earlier views of Hal. He is an admirable politician and a keen quester who seeks glory and power. Why should he not? He is called to that condition. Falstaff's calling is to a more abundant life, however sleazy. But all dispraise of Falstaff merely shows how much he can spare. Freedom and Falstaff might be the motto we carry into the battle of our lives.

Rosalie Colie, a dear friend, was an incisive reader of Shakespeare. In one of our discussions she told me that Falstaff's function was to humanize Hal. She also suggested that, despite appearances, Falstaff and Hal were surprisingly alike, since each evaded responsibility with considerable pleasure. In flight from the court, Hal found in Falstaff a substantial reality away from a time that the Prince knew nevertheless would reclaim him.

There is something in Colie's argument, though, as she acknowledged, the overwhelming effect of Falstaff upon the stage voided the historical reality of Henry V. Shakespeare knew how complex a task he had taken on by opposing his fictive creation Falstaff to the history of English Kings in the fifteenth century. Falstaff wins. Just as Hamlet sustains our illusion that he is an actual person surrounded by so many puppets, Falstaff seems real and all the other roles are roles. When Falstaff enters, something in me murmurs:

Let be be finale of seem.
The only emperor is the emperor of ice-cream.

Wallace Stevens

What chance have Henry IV and Henry V against the "emperor of ice-cream"? Perhaps ice cream, had Sir John lived in the sixteenth century, would have replaced sherris sack for him. He would have become even fatter and unhealthier, but sack would have been less appropriate for Falstaff than ice cream. In one of his myriad aspects, Sir John is an overgrown child. On his death-bed, he becomes a child again, playing with flowers and smiling at his fingertips.

CHAPTER 12

Ancient Pistol
and Doll Tearsheet

Disguising themselves as waiters (drawers), the Prince and Poins
prepare a jollification in which they will eavesdrop on Falstaff and
the vehement whore Doll Tearsheet. Doll is high on Canary wine,
an excessively sweet potion I recommend to no one. Falstaff enters
singing a distorted version of the ballad "Sir Lancelot du Lake."
Their dialogue, punctuated by Mistress Quickly's malapropisms,
shows that for a moment Doll can hold her own with Sir John:

Mistress Quickly: I' faith, sweetheart, methinks now you are
 in an excellent good temperality. Your pulsidge beats as
 extraordinarily as heart would desire, and your colour I
 warrant you is as red as any rose, in good truth, la! But,
 i' faith you have drunk too much canaries, and that's a
 marvellous searching wine, and it perfumes the blood ere
 one can say, 'What's this?' How do you now?
Doll Tearsheet: Better than I was—hem!
Mistress Quickly: Why, that's well said—a good heart's worth
 gold. Lo, here comes Sir John.
[Enter Falstaff, singing.]
Falstaff: 'When Arthur first in court'—Empty the jordan.—
 'And was a worthy king'—How now, Mistress Doll?
Mistress Quickly: Sick of a calm; yea, good faith.

83

Falstaff: So is all her sect; and they be once in a calm they are sick.

Doll Tearsheet: A pox damn you, you muddy rascal, is that all the comfort you give me?

Falstaff: You make fat rascals, Mistress Doll.

Doll Tearsheet: I make them! Gluttony and diseases make them, I make them not.

Falstaff: If the cook help to make the gluttony, you help to make the diseases, Doll; we catch of you, Doll, we catch of you; grant that, my poor virtue, grant that.

Doll Tearsheet: Yea, joy, our chains and our jewels.

Falstaff: 'Your brooches, pearls, and ouches'—for to serve bravely is to come halting off, you know; to come off the breach, with his pike bent bravely; and to surgery bravely; to venture upon the charged chambers bravely;—

Doll Tearsheet: Hang yourself, you muddy conger, hang yourself!

Mistress Quickly: By my troth, this is the old fashion; you two never meet but you fall to some discord. You are both, i' good truth, as rheumatic as two dry toasts, you cannot one bear with another's confirmities. What the goodyear! One must bear, [*to Doll*] and that must be you—you are the weaker vessel, as they say, the emptier vessel.

Doll Tearsheet: Can a weak empty vessel bear such a huge full hogs-head? There's a whole merchant's venture of Bourdeaux stuff in him; you have not seen a hulk better stuffed in the hold. Come, I'll be friends with thee, Jack, thou art going to the wars, and whether I shall ever see thee again or no there is nobody cares.

Henry IV, Part 2, act 2, scene 4, lines 22–66

Quite aside from the continuous sexual innuendoes, this exchange delights as two carousers highlight the festivity of flesh. Mistress Quickly cannot keep her humors straight and means "choleric" when she says "rheumatic." The boisterous scene augments with the arrival of Ancient Pistol the Roaring Boy, a street hoodlum adept at annoying passersby but harmless except for the noise:

> Falstaff: Welcome, Ancient Pistol. Here, Pistol, I charge you with a cup of sack; do you discharge upon mine hostess.
> Pistol: I will discharge upon her, Sir John, with two bullets.
> Falstaff: She is pistol-proof, sir; you shall not hardly offend her.
> Mistress Quickly: Come, I'll drink no proofs, nor no bullets; I'll drink no more than will do me good, for no man's pleasure, I.
> Pistol: Then to you, Mistress Dorothy! I will charge you.
> Doll Tearsheet: Charge me! I scorn you, scurvy companion. What, you poor, base, rascally, cheating, lack-linen mate! Away, you mouldy rogue, away! I am meat for your master.
> Pistol: I know you, Mistress Dorothy.
> Doll Tearsheet: Away, you cut-purse rascal, you filthy bung, away! By this wine, I'll thrust my knife in your mouldy chaps, and you play saucy cuttle with me. Away, you bottle-ale rascal, you basket-hilt stale juggler, you! Since when, I pray you, sir? God's light, with two points on your shoulder? Much!
> Pistol: God let me not live, but I will murder your ruff for this.
> Falstaff: No more, Pistol! I would not have you go off here. Discharge yourself of our company, Pistol.

Mistress Quickly: No, good Captain Pistol, not here, sweet captain.

Doll Tearsheet: Captain! Thou abominable damned cheater, art thou not ashamed to be called captain? And captains were of my mind, they would truncheon you out, for taking their names upon you before you have earned them. You a captain? You slave! For what? For tearing a poor whore's ruff in a bawdy-house? He a captain? Hang him, rogue, he lives upon mouldy stewed prunes and dried cakes. A captain? God's light, these villains will make the word as odious as the word 'occupy', which was an excellent good word before it was ill sorted: therefore captains had need look to't.

act 2, scene 4, lines 109–47

Pistol's rant turns theatrical as Shakespeare satirizes the playwrights George Peele, Thomas Kyd, and most strikingly Christopher Marlowe. In the second part of *Tamburlaine the Great* the victorious hero whips the captive kings dragging his chariot and cries out: "Holla, ye pamper'd jades of Asia! / What, can ye draw but twenty miles a day?" Pistol mangles this with his "hollow pamper'd jades of Asia." When he rhetorically declaims "Have we not Hiren here?" that curious "Hiren" is his iron sword, which he can display but hardly use. His exclamation points and self-answering questions are too much for the formidable Doll, who prompts Falstaff to thrust at Pistol's shoulder and drive him down into the street.

It delights me that Doll Tearsheet protests the debasement of the word "occupy," made odious when given prurient meaning. Shakespeare and Ben Jonson were friends and rivals; perhaps in conversation Jonson complained against the obscene appropriation of a proper and fit word like "occupy," as he was to do in his

86

Timber or Discoveries published in 1640, three years after his death. It would be like Shakespeare slyly to have his boisterous slattern prophesy Jonson's learned disapproval.

Ancient Pistol is a riot of language run wild. He is a parody of a parody, going from nonsense to an irreality, as though his empty head is a parcel of fustian tags from third-rate contemporary dramas. He cries out "Then feed and be fat, my fair Calipolis!" quoting a splendid moment in George Peele's *Battle of Alcazar* where one Muly Mahamet comes on stage with lion flesh on his sword and gives it to his starving mother Calypolis. Pistol garbles everything he approaches as with his "*Si fortune me tormente sperato me contento.*" This renders as "If fortune torments me, hope contents me," but the language is a mix of Spanish and Italian. His "And are etceteras nothings?" can be read as sexual innuendo yet there is a nihilistic undersong that is scarcely Pistol's own.

You cannot be one of Falstaff's crew and continue to speak in your own voice, such as it is. The empty-minded Pistol has been contaminated not just by Falstaff's language but also by the Fat Knight's hidden dread of the abyss of rejection and death. What does Falstaff think of Pistol? He finds that Roaring Boy diverting enough, though with an amiable contempt he recognizes the cowardice and absurdity of the rascal.

Before the Ancient is thrust downstairs by Falstaff he shouts out: "Then death rock me asleep, abridge my doleful days!" Shakespeare's audience might be expected to recognize this as a fragment from a poem either by Anne Boleyn or by her brother George as they awaited execution by Henry VIII in 1536:

Bardolph: Pray thee go down, good ancient.
Falstaff: Hark thee hither, Mistress Doll.
Pistol: Not I! I tell thee what, Corporal Bardolph, I could tear her! I'll be revenged of her.

Page: Pray thee go down.

Pistol: I'll see her damned first! To Pluto's damnèd lake, by this
hand, to th' infernal deep, with Erebus and tortures vile
also! Hold hook and line, say I! Down, down, dogs! Down,
faitors! Have we not Hiren here? [*Draws his sword.*]

Mistress Quickly: Good Captain Peesel, be quiet; 'tis very late,
i' faith I beseek you now, aggravate your choler.

Pistol: These be good humours, indeed! Shall pack-horses,
And hollow pamper'd jades of Asia,
Which cannot go but thirty mile a day,
Compare with Caesars and with Cannibals,
And Troyant Greeks? Nay, rather damn them with
King Cerberus, and let the welkin roar!
Shall we fall foul for toys?

Mistress Quickly: By my troth, captain, these are very bitter
words.

Bardolph: Be gone, good ancient; this will grow to a brawl anon.

Pistol: Die men like dogs! Give crowns like pins! Have we not
Hiren here?

Mistress Quickly: O' my word, captain, there's none such here.
What the goodyear, do you think I would deny her? For
God's sake, be quiet.

Pistol: Then feed and be fat, my fair Calipolis!
Come, give's some sack.
Si fortune me tormente sperato me contento.
Fear we broadsides? No, let the fiend give fire!
Give me some sack; and, sweetheart, lie thou there!
[*Lays down his sword.*]
Come we to full points here? And are etceteras nothings?

Falstaff: Pistol, I would be quiet.

Pistol: Sweet knight, I kiss thy neaf. What! we have seen the
seven stars.

Doll Tearsheet: For God's sake thrust him downstairs, I
    cannot endure such a fustian rascal.

Pistol: Thrust him downstairs? Know we not Galloway nags?

Falstaff: Quoit him down, Bardolph, like a shove-groat
    shilling. Nay, an a' do nothing but speak nothing, a' shall
    be nothing here.

Bardolph: Come, get you downstairs.

Pistol: What! shall we have incision? Shall we imbrue?
    [*Snatches up his sword.*]
    Then death rock me asleep, abridge my doleful days!
    Why, then, let grievous, ghastly, gaping wounds
    Untwine the Sisters Three! Come, Atropos, I say!

Mistress Quickly: Here's goodly stuff toward!

Falstaff: Give me my rapier, boy.

Doll Tearsheet: I pray thee, Jack, I pray thee, do not draw.

Falstaff: [*Drawing*] Get you downstairs.

Mistress Quickly: Here's a goodly tumult! I'll foreswear
    keeping house afore I'll be in these tirrits and frights!
    [*Falstaff thrusts at Pistol.*] So! Murder, I warrant now!
    Alas, alas, put up your naked weapons, put up your naked
    weapons. [*Exit Bardolph, driving Pistol out.*]

                         act 2, scene 4, lines 148–204

With Pistol discharged we move to a moment grotesque,
pathetic, and yet curiously touched by a fine melancholy:

Doll Tearsheet: Ah, you sweet little rogue, you! Alas, poor
    ape, how thou sweat'st! Come, let me wipe thy face.
    Come on, you whoreson chops! Ah, rogue! i'faith, I love
    thee. Thou art as valorous as Hector of Troy, worth five
    of Agamemnon, and ten times better than the Nine
    Worthies. Ah, villain!

Falstaff: A rascally slave! I will toss the rogue in a blanket.

Doll Tearsheet: Do, an thou dar'st for thy heart. And thou
dost, I'll canvass thee between a pair of sheets.

[*Enter musicians.*]

Page: The music is come, sir.

Falstaff: Let them play. Play, sirs! Sit on my knee, Doll. A
rascal bragging slave! The rogue fled from me like
quicksilver.

Doll Tearsheet: I'faith, and thou followedst him like a church.
Thou whoreson little tidy Bartholomew boar-pig, when
wilt thou leave fighting a-days and foining a-nights, and
begin to patch up thine old body for heaven?

[*Enter (, behind,) the Prince and Poins disguised (as drawers).*]

Falstaff: Peace, good Doll! Do not speak like a death's-head;
do not bid me remember mine end.

act 2, scene 4, lines 215–32

Shuddering at the vision of a memento mori or mute yet vocif-
erous skull, Falstaff recoils. He finds relief in demeaning Hal and
Poins, eavesdroppers who are moved to near-violence:

Falstaff: Thou dost give me flattering busses.

Doll Tearsheet: By my troth, I kiss thee with a most constant
heart.

Falstaff: I am old, I am old.

Doll Tearsheet: I love thee better than I love e'er a scurvy
young boy of them all.

Falstaff: What stuff wilt have a kirtle of? I shall receive money
a-Thursday, shalt have a cap tomorrow. A merry song!
Come, it grows late, we'll to bed. Thou't forget me when
I am gone.

Doll Tearsheet: By my troth, thou't set me a-weeping, and thou sayst so. Prove that ever I dress myself handsome till thy return,—Well, hearken a' th' end.

From low comedy, Shakespeare moves us to the pathos of Falstaff acknowledging his age, and seeking the bought affection of a whore to divert him from what he knows will come. I read this and sorrow like rain falls upon me.

With the entrance of Hal and Poins, the mood shifts:

Falstaff: Some sack, Francis.

Hal: [*With Poins, coming forward*] Anon, anon, sir.

Falstaff: Ha! A bastard son of the King's? And art not thou Poins his brother?

Hal: Why, thou globe of sinful continents, what a life dost thou lead!

Falstaff: A better than thou—I am a gentleman, thou art a drawer.

Hal: Very true, sir, and I come to draw you out by the ears.

Mistress Quickly: O the Lord preserve thy good Grace! By my troth, welcome to London! Now the Lord bless that sweet face of thine! O Jesu, are you come from Wales?

Falstaff: Thou whoreson mad compound of majesty, by this light flesh and corrupt blood [*leaning his hand upon Doll*], thou art welcome.

Doll Tearsheet: How! You fat fool, I scorn you.

Poins: My lord, he will drive you out of your revenge and turn all to a merriment, if you take not the heat.

Hal: You whoreson candle-mine you, how vilely did you speak of me even now, before this honest, virtuous, civil gentlewoman!

Mistress Quickly: God's blessing of your good heart! and so
she is, by my troth.

act 2, scene 4, lines 266–301

There is a kind of genial glow suffusing this scene. It is the only time in *Part 2* before the rejection of Falstaff that Hal and Sir John are together. Their banter back and forth has something of the joyous exchanges in *Part 1*. The edge of the Prince's aggressivity sharpens though he participates in the merriment. Falstaff is in high form in his mock-judgment of Doll and Mistress Quickly: "For one of them, she's in hell already and burns poor souls. For th' other, I owe her money, and whether she be damned for that I know not."

A knock at the door, recalling the end of Falstaff and Hal playing Henry IV and the Prince in alternation, returns us to the universe of rebellion. When the Prince asks for his sword and cloak, he speaks his only civil words in farewell: "Falstaff, good night." At that moment only is there the illusion of harmony between them.

CHAPTER 13

Uneasy Lies the Head
That Wears a Crown

The historical King Henry IV had a troubled reign marked by a series of rebellions. These form the political and military aspects of both parts of *Henry IV*. Shakespeare, as might be expected, creates a king of considerable sensitivity so humanized that he compels us to a curious compassion. His soliloquy lamenting his sleeplessness is eloquent and memorable, and few can hear it without sympathy:

> How many thousands of my poorest subjects
> Are at this hour asleep! O sleep, O gentle sleep,
> Nature's soft nurse, how have I frightened thee,
> That thou no more will weigh my eyelids down,
> And steep my senses in forgetfulness?
> Why rather, sleep, liest thou in smoky cribs,
> Upon uneasy pallets stretching thee,
> And hush'd with buzzing night-flies to thy slumber,
> Than in the perfum'd chambers of the great,
> Under the canopies of costly state,
> And lull'd with sound of sweetest melody?
> O thou dull god, why liest thou with the vile
> In loathsome beds, and leav'st the kingly couch
> A watch-case or a common 'larum-bell?
> Wilt thou upon the high and giddy mast

Seal up the ship-boy's eyes, and rock his brains
In cradle of the rude imperious surge,
And in the visitation of the winds,
Who take the ruffian billows by the top,
Curling their monstrous heads, and hanging them
With deafing clamour in the slippery clouds,
That with the hurly death itself awakes?
Canst thou, O partial sleep, give thy repose
To the wet sea-boy in an hour so rude;
And in the calmest and most stillest night,
With all appliances and means to boot,
Deny it to a king? Then, happy low, lie down!
Uneasy lies the head that wears a crown.

Henry IV, Part 2, act 3, scene 1, lines 4–31

Matthew Arnold chose as one of his touchstones:

Wilt thou upon the high and giddy mast
Seal up the ship-boy's eyes, and rock his brains
In cradle of the rude imperious surge. . . .

Shakespeare alludes to Proverbs 23:34: "Yea, thou shalt be as he that lieth down in the midst of the sea, or as he that lieth upon the top of a mast." The image of precariousness is vivid and expresses both the King's insomnia and his exposed situation as usurper and regicide. In a further lament Henry IV seems to echo or presage Shakespeare's Sonnet 64:

When I have seen by Time's fell hand defaced
The rich proud cost of outworn buried age;
When sometime lofty towers I see down-razed
And brass eternal slave to mortal rage;

When I have seen the hungry ocean gain
Advantage on the kingdom of the shore,
And the firm soil win of the watery main,
Increasing store with loss and loss with store;
When I have seen such interchange of state,
Or state itself confounded to decay;
Ruin hath taught me thus to ruminate,
That Time will come and take my love away.
     This thought is as a death, which cannot choose
     But weep to have that which it fears to lose.

King Henry IV's lament pierces us with more intense plangency:

O God! that one might read the book of fate,
And see the revolution of the times
Make mountains level, and the continent,
Weary of solid firmness, melt itself
Into the sea; and other times to see
The beachy girdle of the ocean
Too wide for Neptune's hips; how chances mock,
And changes fill the cup of alteration
With divers liquors! O, if this were seen,
The happiest youth, viewing his progress through,
What perils past, what crosses to ensue,
Would shut the book and sit him down and die.
                    act 3, scene 1, lines 45–56

It is very likely that Shakespeare the actor spoke these lines in performance. Certainly Henry IV is not his surrogate but one wonders if we are not listening to William Shakespeare meditating on the revolution of the times. The wealth of the *Henry IV* plays is so opulent that even the usurper king speaks to the heart of our sorrow. His lament applies not only to his time and Shakespeare's, but to our frightening moment of climate change.

The Henry V of history had a vexed political relation to his father Henry IV. It is possible that he may have planned a coup to assume power. Certainly in 1411 Henry IV dismissed his son from the council of advisors, a drastic move since throughout 1410 the Prince headed the court during his father's illness. Shakespeare alters history so that father and son share an affection tempered by their mutual drive toward ascendancy. Though Hal is beyond his father in imagination and in charisma, he remains recognizably the usurper's son. Kingship enthralls them both.

When Henry IV seems dead in his sleep, the Prince prematurely crowns himself:

Why doth the crown lie there upon his pillow,
Being so troublesome a bedfellow?
O polish'd perturbation! golden care!
That keep'st the ports of slumber open wide
To many a watchful night! Sleep with it now:
Yet not so sound, and half so deeply sweet,
As he whose brow with homely biggen bound
Snores out the watch of night. O majesty!
When thou dost pinch thy bearer, thou dost sit
Like a rich armour worn in heat of day,
That scald'st with safety. By his gates of breath
There lies a downy feather which stirs not.
Did he suspire, that light and weightless down
Perforce must move. My gracious lord! My father!
This sleep is sound indeed; this is a sleep
That from this golden rigol hath divorc'd
So many English kings. Thy due from me

Is tears and heavy sorrows of the blood,
Which nature, love, and filial tenderness
Shall, O dear father, pay thee plenteously.
My due from thee is this imperial crown,
Which, as immediate from thy place and blood,
Derives itself to me. [*Putting it on his head*] Lo here it sits,
Which God shall guard; and put the world's whole strength
Into one giant arm, it shall not force
This lineal honour from me. This from thee
Will I to mine leave as 'tis left to me. [*Exit.*]

            act 4, scene 5, lines 20–46

It is a little difficult to estimate the extent of Hal's premature grief. He rather hastily postpones the tears he *will* shed when he has time. The Prince's passion is evoked by the imperial crown, which he is happy to place on his own head. His emphasis is on his lineal legitimacy and on the inception of his status as hero-king. With that he exits, Henry IV awakens, and demands his missing crown. His understandable fury will be assuaged, though again one wonders at the report that Hal has been discovered gently weeping away. Their exchange is an epitome of their mutual nature:

Prince Henry: I never thought to hear you speak again.
King Henry IV: Thy wish was father, Harry, to that thought;
I stay too long by thee, I weary thee.
Dost thou so hunger for mine empty chair
That thou wilt needs invest thee with my honours
Before thy hour be ripe? O foolish youth!
Thou seek'st the greatness that will overwhelm thee.
Stay but a little, for my cloud of dignity
Is held from falling with so weak a wind
That it will quickly drop; my day is dim.

Thou hast stol'n that which after some few hours
Were thine without offence, and at my death
Thou hast seal'd up my expectation.
                              act 4, scene 5, lines 91–103

The rejection and death of Sir John Falstaff hovers close by. Hal's response is a little hard to absorb without considerable irony: "The noble change that I have purposed!" Reconciled, Henry IV treats his heir to politic advice:

Therefore, my Harry,
Be it thy course to busy giddy minds
With foreign quarrels, that action, hence borne out
May waste the memory of the former days.
More would I, but my lungs are wasted so
That strength of speech is utterly denied me.
How I came by the crown, O God forgive,
And grant it may with thee in true peace live!
                              act 4, scene 5, lines 212–19

The campaign against France in *The Life of King Henry the Fifth* is thus prophesied. Whether we are moved by the King's dying remorse for his murder of King Richard II is a question Shakespeare yields up to our judgment.

Sir John Falstaff has no place in the long deviation of Prince Hal from the court, and many playgoers and readers join me in feeling a degree of malaise as one hypocrite affectionately hands off the crown to another. Shakespeare's detachment is absolute. We cannot know whether he longs to get Falstaff back on stage. Nevertheless the return of Sir John is, as it should be, outrageously refreshing.

CHAPTER 14

Shallow and Silence: Falstaff at Recruitment

Falstaff outweighs all but the most searing of Shakespeare's personalities: Hamlet, Iago, Lear, Macbeth, Cleopatra, Shylock. The *Henry IV* plays abound in extraordinary characterizations: Hal, Hotspur, King Henry IV, Mistress Quickly, Doll Tearsheet, Ancient Pistol, and Justice Robert Shallow.

Shakespeare invents the new kind of comedy we have learned to call nonsense when we enter the world of Justice Shallow and his kinsman Justice Silence:

Shallow: Come on, come on, come on: give me your hand, sir,
  give me your hand, sir; an early stirrer, by the rood! And
  how doth my good cousin Silence?
Silence: Good morrow, good cousin Shallow.
Shallow: And how doth my cousin, your bedfellow? and your
  fairest daughter and mine, my god-daughter Ellen?
Silence: Alas, a black woosel, cousin Shallow!
Shallow: By yea and no, sir: I dare say my cousin William is
  become a good scholar; he is at Oxford still, is he not?
Silence: Indeed, sir, to my cost.
Shallow: A' must, then, to the Inns o'Court shortly: I was once
  of Clement's Inn, where I think they will talk of mad
  Shallow yet.

Silence: You were called 'lusty Shallow' then, cousin.

Shallow: By the mass, I was called anything, and I would have done anything indeed too, and roundly too. There was I, and little John Doit of Staffordshire, and black George Barnes, and Francis Pickbone, and Will Squele, a Cotsole man—you had not four such swinge-bucklers in all the Inns o'Court again; and I may say to you, we knew where the bona-robas were, and had the best of them all at commandment. Then was Jack Falstaff, now Sir John, a boy, and page to Thomas Mowbray, Duke of Norfolk.

Silence: This Sir John, cousin, that comes hither anon about soldiers?

Shallow: The same Sir John, the very same. I see him break Scoggin's head at the court-gate, when a' was a crack, not thus high; and the very same day did I fight with one Sampson Stockfish, a fruiterer, behind Gray's Inn. Jesu, Jesu, the mad days that I have spent! And to see how many of my old acquaintance are dead!

Silence: We shall all follow, cousin.

Shallow: Certain, 'tis certain, very sure, very sure. Death, as the Psalmist saith, is certain to all, all shall die. How a good yoke of bullocks at Stamford fair?

Silence: By my troth, I was not there.

Shallow: Death is certain. Is old Double of your town living yet?

Silence: Dead, sir.

Shallow: Jesu, Jesu, dead! A' drew a good bow, and dead! A' shot a fine shoot: John a Gaunt loved him well, and betted much money on his head. Dead! A' would have clapped i'th'clout at twelve score, and carried you a forehand shaft a fourteen and fourteen and a half, that it

would have done a man's heart good to see. How a score
of ewes now?

Silence: Thereafter as they be; a score of good ewes may be
worth ten pounds.

Shallow: And is old Double dead?

Henry IV, Part 2, act 3, scene 2, lines 1–52

My Shallow is Laurence Olivier's. Uncannily Olivier precisely
exemplified Falstaff's marvelous description of Justice Robert
Shallow as a forked radish, as lecherous as a monkey, so that the
whores called him mandrake:

Now Reuben went in the days of the wheat harvest, and found
mandrakes in the field, and brought them unto his mother
Leah. Then said Rachel to Leah, Give me, I pray thee, of thy
son's mandrakes.

But she answered her, Is it a small matter for thee to take
mine husband, except thou take my son's mandrakes also? Then
said Rachel, Therefore he shall sleep with thee this night for thy
son's mandrakes.

And Jacob came from the field in the evening, and Leah
went out to meet him, and said, Come in to me, for I have
bought and paid for thee with my son's mandrakes: and he slept
with her that night.

Genesis 30:14–16, Geneva Bible 1599

The marginal gloss in the Geneva Bible rendition of the story
of Leah and the Mandrakes reads: "Which is a kind of herb whose
root hath a certain likeness of the figure of a man." Traditionally
the mandrake represented male sexual fervor as in John Donne's
"Song":

Go and catch a falling star,
  Get with child a mandrake root,
Tell me where all past years are,
  Or who cleft the Devil's foot,
Teach me to hear mermaids singing,
  Or to keep off envy's stinging,
      And find
      What wind
Serves to advance an honest mind.

The harlots manifested Falstaffian wit in calling the starveling Shallow a mandrake. Shakespeare is not Falstaff even if Falstaff is Shakespeare. Shallow has a touch of ridiculous pathos in his monotonous garrulity. Silence prompts Shallow's loquacity with the absurd appellation of "lusty Shallow." We grimace at a swashbuckling Shallow who frequented the bona-robas, neatly defined by Dr. Johnson as "fine showy wantons." But then we are alerted by reference to Falstaff as a rough boy breaking the head of one Scoggin. An odd alternation of the price of livestock and of human mortality heightens the nonsense until the antiphony of the price of ewes and the death of old Double.

Falstaff makes a grand entrance:

Falstaff: I am glad to see you well, good Master Robert
  Shallow. Master Surecard, as I think?
Shallow: No, Sir John, it is my cousin Silence, in commission
  with me.
Falstaff: Good Master Silence, it well befits you should be of
  the peace.
Silence: Your good worship is welcome.
Falstaff: Fie, this is hot weather, gentlemen. Have you
  provided me here half a dozen sufficient men?

Shallow: Marry have we, sir. Will you sit?

Falstaff: Let me see them, I beseech you.

The Fat Knight sets the tone with his deliberate mistake of "Surecard" for "Shallow," and follows with the jest that a judge named "Silence" is indeed a Justice of the Peace. "Sufficient men" is another Falstaffian quibble since he uses the archaic sense of "competent" or "qualified," while implying they are to buy themselves out and so be sufficient for his perpetually needy financial condition:

> Shallow: Where's the roll? where's the roll? where's the roll?
>   Let me see, let me see, let me see. So, so, so, so, so, so. So.
>   Yea, marry, sir: Rafe Mouldy! Let them appear as I call; let
>   them do so, let them do so. Let me see; where is Mouldy?
> Mouldy: Here, and't please you.
> Shallow: What think you, Sir John? A good-limbed fellow,
>   young, strong, and of good friends.
> Falstaff: Is thy name Mouldy?
> Mouldy: Yea, and't please you.
> Falstaff: 'Tis the more time thou wert used.
> Shallow: Ha, ha, ha! most excellent, i'faith, things that are
>   mouldy lack use: Very singular good, in faith, well said,
>   Sir John, very well said.
> Falstaff: Prick him.
> Mouldy: I was pricked well enough before, an you could have
>   let me alone. My old dame will be undone now for one to
>   do her husbandry and her drudgery. You need not to have
>   pricked me, there are other men fitter to go out than I.
> Falstaff: Go to; peace, Mouldy; you shall go, Mouldy; it is time
>   you were spent.
> Mouldy: Spent!

Falstaff's rich word "prick" intends a myriad of meanings: the archaic "rouse" or "urge on"; the marking for impressment into the King's army; the obscene sense of penetration. The wretched Mouldy is to be used up but with the innuendo that he can save himself by spending Falstaff's bribe.

The unfortunate Simon Shadow, who seems penniless, spurs Falstaff's darkening wit. Heartlessly Sir John, who sweats profusely in sunlight, pricks Shadow as a shade to sit under:

Shallow: Peace, fellow, peace—stand aside; know you where you are? For th'other, Sir John—let me see: Simon Shadow!

Falstaff: Yea, marry, let me have him to sit under. He's like to be a cold soldier. . . .

Shallow: Thomas Wart!

Falstaff: Where's he?

Wart: Here, sir.

Falstaff: Is thy name Wart?

Wart: Yea, sir.

Falstaff: Thou art a very ragged Wart.

Shallow: Shall I prick him, Sir John?

Falstaff: It were superfluous, for his apparel is built upon his back, and the whole frame stands upon pins: prick him no more.

The ragged Wart, diminutive and blemished, is dismissed since one prick and he would come down. Feeble, unexpectedly valiant, provokes Falstaff to a crescendo of mounting nonsense:

Shallow: Francis Feeble!

Feeble: Here, sir.

Falstaff: What trade art thou, Feeble?

Feeble: A woman's tailor, sir.

Shallow: Shall I prick him, sir?

Falstaff: You may; but if he had been a man's tailor, he'd
ha' pricked you. Wilt thou make as many holes in an
enemy's battle as thou hast done in a woman's petticoat?

Feeble: I will do my good will, sir; you can have no more.

Falstaff: Well said, good woman's tailor! well said, courageous
Feeble! Thou wilt be as valiant as the wrathful dove or
most magnanimous mouse. Prick the woman's tailor:
well, Master Shallow; deep, Master Shallow.

. . .

Falstaff: Who is next?

Shallow: Peter Bullcalf o'th'green!

. . .

Bullcalf: O Lord, sir! I am a diseased man.

Falstaff: What disease hast thou?

Bullcalf: A whoreson cold, sir, a cough, sir, which I caught
with ringing in the King's affairs upon his coronation
day, sir.

Falstaff: Come, thou shalt go to the wars in a gown

. . .

Shallow: I pray you, go in with me to dinner.

Falstaff: Come, I will go drink with you, but I cannot tarry
dinner. I am glad to see you, by my troth, Master
Shallow.

Shallow: O, Sir John, do you remember since we lay all night
in the Windmill in Saint George's Field?

Falstaff: No more of that, good Master Shallow, no more of
that.

Shallow: Ha, 'twas a merry night! And is Jane Nightwork
alive?

Falstaff: She lives, Master Shallow.

Shallow: She never could away with me.

Falstaff: Never, never; she would always say she could not abide Master Shallow.

Shallow: By the mass, I could anger her to th' heart. She was then a bona-roba. Doth she hold her own well?

Falstaff: Old, old, Master Shallow.

Shallow: Nay, she must be old, she cannot choose but be old, certain she's old, and had Robin Nightwork by old Nightwork before I came to Clement's Inn.

Silence: That's fifty-five year ago.

Shallow: Ha, cousin Silence, that thou hadst seen that that this knight and I have seen! Ha, Sir John, said I well?

Falstaff: We have heard the chimes at midnight, Master Shallow.

act 3, scene 2, lines 85–210

"Surecard" is Sir John's witty assessment of Silence and Shallow, both "safe bets" ripe for extortion. The unfortunate recruits bear the appropriate names: Mouldy, Shadow, Wart, Feeble, and Bullcalf. Falstaff robustly pricks or lists each in turn: Mouldy needs use; Shadow will be another of fictive names to augment Sir John's pockets; Wart, who is spared since he would come tumbling down; the surprising Feeble as valiant as an angry dove or a strong-hearted mouse. Last comes Bullcalf and Falstaff pricks him expecting a roar. Poor Bullcalf protests his cough to no avail.

Sir John's rather poignant regard for Shallow's dignity allows him to humor the starveling mandrake with the magnificent reverberation of: "We have heard the chimes at midnight, Master Shallow." Orson Welles with consummate taste took the title of his motion picture exalting Falstaff from the luminous suggestion of that strong line.

Shakespeare, keenly aware of the richness in the contrast of Shallow and Falstaff, prolongs the scene of recruitment:

Bullcalf: Good Master Corporate Bardolph, stand my friend; and here's four Harry ten shillings in French crowns for you. In very truth, sir, I had as lief be hanged, sir, as go: and yet, for mine own part, sir, I do not care; but rather, because I am unwilling, and, for mine own part, have a desire to stay with my friends; else, sir, I did not care, for mine own part, so much.

Bardolph: Go to; stand aside.

Mouldy: And, good master corporal captain, for my old dame's sake, stand my friend: she has nobody to do any thing about her when I am gone; and she is old, and cannot help herself: You shall have forty, sir.

Bardolph: Go to; stand aside.

. . .

[Re-enter Falstaff and the Justices.]

Falstaff: Come, sir, which men shall I have?

Shallow: Four of which you please.

Bardolph: Sir, a word with you: I have three pound to free Mouldy and Bullcalf.

Falstaff: Go to; well.

Shallow: Come, Sir John, which four will you have?

Falstaff: Do you choose for me.

Shallow: Marry, then, Mouldy, Bullcalf, Feeble and Shadow.

Falstaff: Mouldy and Bullcalf: for you, Mouldy, stay at home till you are past service: and for your part, Bullcalf, grow till you come unto it: I will none of you.

Shallow: Sir John, Sir John, do not yourself wrong: they are your likeliest men, and I would have you served with the best.

Falstaff: Will you tell me, Master Shallow, how to choose a
man? Care I for the limb, the thewes, the stature, bulk,
and big assemblance of a man! Give me the spirit,
Master Shallow. Here's Wart; you see what a ragged
appearance it is; a' shall charge you and discharge you
with the motion of a pewterer's hammer, come off and
on swifter than he that gibbets on the brewer's bucket.
And this same half-faced fellow, Shadow; give me this
man: he presents no mark to the enemy; the foeman
may with as great aim level at the edge of a penknife.
And for a retreat; how swiftly will this Feeble the
woman's tailor run off! O, give me the spare men, and
spare me the great ones. Put me a caliver into Wart's
hand, Bardolph.
Bardolph: Hold, Wart, traverse; thus, thus, thus.
Falstaff: Come, manage me your caliver. So: very well: go to:
very good, exceeding good. O, give me always a little,
lean, old, chapt, bald shot. . . .

act 3, scene 2, lines 215–70

Falstaff mocks military theory and practice with the zest and
gusto we come to expect from the personality most rammed
with life in all Shakespeare. Mouldy and Bullcalf, having bought
themselves off, are dismissed, to Shallow's consternation. Whenever I teach Henry V's patriotic rant at Agincourt, a voice within
me repeats Falstaff's prophetic parody: "Give me the spirit." The
wretched Wart is commended for swiftness, poor Shadow for presenting no target, and Feeble for his rapidity in retreat.

Wart's training consists of marching up and down with a carbine after which Falstaff happily counterfeits the military nonsense of his era that assigned tall men for the pike and little fellows
for the musket.

Falstaff, after ridding himself of Shallow and Silence, concludes with a grand soliloquy:

As I return, I will fetch off these justices: I do see the bottom of Justice Shallow. Lord, Lord, how subject we old men are to this vice of lying! This same starved justice hath done nothing but prate to me of the wildness of his youth, and the feats he hath done about Turnbull Street: and every third word a lie, duer paid to the hearer than the Turk's tribute. I do remember him at Clement's Inn like a man made after supper of a cheese-paring: when a' was naked, he was, for all the world, like a forked radish, with a head fantastically carved upon it with a knife: a' was so forlorn, that his dimensions to any thick sight were invincible: a' was the very genius of famine; yet lecherous as a monkey, and the whores called him mandrake: a' came ever in the rearward of the fashion, and sung those tunes to the overscutched huswives that he heard the carmen whistle, and swear they were his fancies or his good-nights. And now is this Vice's dagger become a squire, and talks as familiarly of John a Gaunt as if he had been sworn brother to him; and I'll be sworn a' ne'er saw him but once in the tilt-yard; and then he burst his head for crowding among the marshal's men. I saw it, and told John a Gaunt he beat his own name; for you might have thrust him and all his apparel into an eel-skin; the case of a treble hautboy was a mansion for him, a court: and now has he land and beefs. Well, I'll be acquainted with him, if I return; and it shall go hard but I will make him a philosopher's two stones to me: if the young dace be a bait for the old pike, I see no reason in the law of nature but I may snap at him. Let time shape, and there an end.

act 3, scene 2, lines 295–327

When he returns Falstaff will fetch off and fleece Shallow and Silence. Beholding the not very deep bottom of Shallow, Sir John reflects on how old men, a category he now grants includes him, are given to the vice of lying. Turnbull Street was famous for its low hangouts overflowing with whores and thieves. The young Shallow resembled a bifurcated radish, so meager as to be all but invisible. Courting the "overscutched huswives" or freeloader hussies, Shallow sang them tunes picked up from carters and swore they were his own fancies or good nights, that is improvisations.

Somewhat inflating Shallow's wealth, Falstaff resolves to make the eel-skin Justice his dupe. Best of all, Sir John regards Shallow as a dace or small fish to be devoured by the old pike Falstaff. There is a menacing overtone since the dace is young and probably also refers to Prince Hal. Before Sir John returns to Shallow, he makes an enemy of the grim Prince John of Lancaster, Hal's younger brother, who prolongs the perpetual threat of hanging Falstaff from the gallows. If I had to vote for the most unpleasant personality in *Henry IV*, then Prince John wins easily. Praised by Hal for fleshing his maiden sword, Lancaster is the epitome of brutal force and treachery, and so perhaps, the truest son of King Henry IV.

CHAPTER 15

Prince John of Lancaster at Betrayal

Act 4 opens within the forest of Gaultree in Yorkshire, where Lancaster confronts the rebels, who include the Archbishop of York, Mowbray, and Hastings. Shakespeare with Falstaffian irony startles when Lancaster unknowingly echoes Sir John: "You are too shallow, Hastings, much too shallow, / To sound the bottom of the after-times." On one level this means Lancaster's entrapment of the rebels:

> Lancaster: I like them all, and do allow them well,
> And swear here, by the honour of my blood,
> My father's purposes have been mistook,
> And some about him have too lavishly
> Wrested his meaning and authority.
> My lord, these griefs shall be with speed redress'd;
> Upon my soul, they shall. If this may please you,
> Discharge your powers unto their several counties,
> As we will ours: and here between the armies
> Let's drink together friendly and embrace,
> That all their eyes may bear those tokens home
> Of our restored love and amity.
> Archbishop of York: I take your princely word for these
> redresses.

Lancaster: I give it you, and will maintain my word:
And thereupon I drink unto your grace.
Hastings: Go, captain, and deliver to the army
This news of peace: let them have pay, and part:
I know it will well please them. Hie thee, captain.
[*Exit officer.*]

. . .

Lancaster: And let our army be discharged too.
[*Exit Westmoreland.*]
And, good my lord, so please you, let our trains
March, by us, that we may peruse the men
We should have coped withal.
Archbishop of York: Go, good Lord Hastings,
And, ere they be dismissed, let them march by.
[*Exit Hastings.*]
Lancaster: I trust, lords, we shall lie to-night together.
[*Re-enter Westmoreland.*]
Now, cousin, wherefore stands our army still?
Westmoreland: The leaders, having charge from you to stand,
Will not go off until they hear you speak.
Lancaster: They know their duties.
[*Re-enter Hastings.*]
Hastings: My lord, our army is dispersed already;
Like youthful steers unyoked, they take their courses
East, west, north, south; or, like a school broke up,
Each hurries toward his home and sporting-place.
Westmoreland: Good tidings, my Lord Hastings; for the which
I do arrest thee, traitor, of high treason:
And you, lord archbishop, and you, Lord Mowbray,
Of capital treason I attach you both.
Mowbray: Is this proceeding just and honourable?
Westmoreland: Is your assembly so?

Archbishop of York: Will you thus break your faith?

Lancaster: I pawn'd thee none.

act 4, scene 2, lines 54–112

Irony heaps upon irony. There is a chill when Lancaster says "I trust, lords, we shall lie to-night together." The young killer links his honor to "a most Christian care." Presaging King Henry V's giving the glory to God for victory at Agincourt, Lancaster charmingly asserts: "God, and not we, hath safely fought to-day." At least Henry V invokes the God of Battles, while presumably Prince John sees God as the ultimate master of betrayal.

In considerable contrast to Prince John, the tardy Falstaff encounters the rebel Colevile of the Dale:

Falstaff: What's your name, sir? of what condition are you, and of what place, I pray?

Colevile: I am a knight, sir, and my name is Colevile of the Dale.

Falstaff: Well, then, Colevile is your name, a knight is your degree, and your place the Dale: Colevile shall be still your name, a traitor your degree, and the dungeon your place, a place deep enough; so shall you be still Colevile of the Dale.

Colevile: Are not you Sir John Falstaff?

Falstaff: As good a man as he, sir, whoe'er I am. Do ye yield, sir? or shall I sweat for you? if I do sweat, they are the drops of thy lovers, and they weep for thy death: therefore rouse up fear and trembling, and do observance to my mercy.

Colevile: I think you are Sir John Falstaff, and in that thought yield me.

Falstaff: I have a whole school of tongues in this belly of mine,

113

and not a tongue of them all speaks any other word
but my name. And I had but a belly of any indifferency,
I were simply the most active fellow in Europe: my
womb, my womb, my womb, undoes me. Here comes our
general.

act 4, scene 3, lines 1–23

This would be high farce except that Falstaff transfigures the farcical so that it becomes the comedy of language. His belly transcends since all languages speak through it. The wretched Colevile is too cowardly to hold our interest except that he induces our rumination on Sir John's thrice-repeated womb. Prince John of Lancaster enters and resorts to the threatening habit of his family:

Now, Falstaff, where have you been all this while?
When every thing is ended, then you come:
These tardy tricks of yours will, on my life,
One time or other break some gallows' back.

act 4, scene 3, lines 26–29

The subsequent quarrel is a small masterpiece:

Falstaff: I would be sorry, my lord, but it should be thus: I never knew yet but rebuke and cheque was the reward of valour. Do you think me a swallow, an arrow, or a bullet? have I, in my poor and old motion, the expedition of thought? I have speeded hither with the very extremest inch of possibility; I have foundered nine score and odd posts: and here, travel-tainted as I am, have in my pure and immaculate valour, taken Sir John Colevile of the dale, a most furious knight and valorous enemy. But

114

what of that? he saw me, and yielded; that I may justly
say, with the hook-nosed fellow of Rome, three words, 'I
came, saw, and overcame.'

Lancaster: It was more of his courtesy than your deserving.

Falstaff: I know not: here he is, and here I yield him: and
I beseech your grace, let it be booked with the rest
of this day's deeds; or, by the Lord, I will have it in a
particular ballad else, with mine own picture on the top
on't, Colevile kissing my foot: to the which course if I
be enforced, if you do not all show like gilt twopences
to me, and I in the clear sky of fame o'ershine you as
much as the full moon doth the cinders of the element,
which show like pins' heads to her, believe not the word
of the noble: therefore let me have right, and let desert
mount.

Lancaster: Thine's too heavy to mount.

Falstaff: Let it shine, then.

Lancaster: Thine's too thick to shine.

Falstaff: Let it do something, my good lord, that may do me
good, and call it what you will.

act 4, scene 3, lines 30–58

It would be difficult to surpass: "Do you think me a swallow,
an arrow, or a bullet?" Falstaff forces us to think. However poor
and old his motion is, it has the swiftness of his mind. His pure
and immaculate courage has captured Colevile of the Dale, neither furious nor valorous. Falstaff, like Julius Caesar, came, saw, and
overcame. The irate Lancaster denies this achievement and provokes Falstaff to a grand flight of parody: "Therefore let me have
right, and let desert mount." Lancaster, lacking both imagination
and humor, literalizes his insults. Falstaff's merit is too heavy to
mount and too thick to shine. On the contrary the Fat Knight's

merit ascends with agility and outshines Henry IV, Hal, and Lancaster.

Falstaff forever will be the glory of the *Henry IV* plays, yet Hal remains a troubling and eloquent personality, at once a Machiavel and a true spirit who caught fire from Falstaff but then inevitably returned from playing to power.

CHAPTER 16

Falstaff on Sherris Sack

In response to Prince John of Lancaster's parting remark: "I, in my condition, / Shall better speak of you than you deserve," Falstaff delivers a magnificent soliloquy:

I would you had but the wit, 'twere better than your dukedom. Good faith, this same young sober-blooded boy doth not love me; nor a man cannot make him laugh; but that's no marvel, he drinks no wine. There's never none of these demure boys come to any proof; for thin drink doth so over-cool their blood, and making many fish-meals, that they fall into a kind of male green-sickness; and then when they marry, they get wenches: they are generally fools and cowards; which some of us should be too, but for inflammation. A good sherris sack hath a two-fold operation in it. It ascends me into the brain, dries me there all the foolish and dull and curdy vapours which environ it; makes it apprehensive, quick, forgetive, full of nimble fiery and delectable shapes, which, delivered o'er to the voice, the tongue, which is the birth, becomes excellent wit. The second property of your excellent sherris is, the warming of the blood; which, before cold and settled, left the liver white and pale, which is the badge of pusillanimity and cowardice; but the sherris warms it and makes it course from the inwards to the parts extreme: it illumineth the face, which as a beacon gives warning to all the rest of this little kingdom, man, to arm; and then the vital commoners, and inland petty spirits muster me all to their captain, the heart, who, great and puffed up with this retinue, doth any deed of courage; and this valour comes of sherris. So that skill in the weapon is nothing without sack, for that sets it a-work; and learning a mere hoard of gold kept by a devil, till sack commences it and sets it in act and use. Hereof comes it that Prince Harry is valiant; for the cold blood he did naturally inherit of his father, he hath, like lean, sterile and bare land, manured, husbanded and tilled with excellent endeavour of drinking good and good store of fertile sherris, that he is become very hot and valiant. If I had a thousand sons, the first human principle I would teach them should be, to forswear thin potations and to addict themselves to sack.

act 4, scene 3, lines 84–123

Dr. Samuel Johnson commented that Falstaff speaks here like a veteran in life. Despite his moral disapproval of Falstaff, Johnson understood that Falstaff had entered the abyss of himself.

I once believed that Falstaff was free of the superego, of a censor monitoring his aggressivity. I was wrong. His freedom is the actor's freedom, which is to find a role by playing it. Like Cleopatra, Falstaff loves playing. So with a terrible twist does Iago. Hamlet loathes the drama into which he has been thrown. Revenge tragedy for him is as rotten as the state of Denmark. He rebels and creates his own play. Death is his release into the rest of silence. Lear and Macbeth also are released by death. Who would prolong their agony?

Despite the augmenting shadows of rejection, Falstaff continually finds fresh delight in play. As always, it is difficult for me to withstand the temptation of identifying the Fat Knight with Shakespeare himself. In one sense I associate Falstaff with Shakespeare the player, though he certainly never acted that part. Shakespeare the poet-dramatist moves from one superb invention of personality to another and must have known the renewing joy of discovery. It could not have been an unmixed pride and pleasure to inflict upon himself and us the shattering of Lear and his world. After the composition of *Macbeth* there may have been a withdrawal from the journey into chaos.

Falstaff though was a liberation. He seems to have leaped into the *Henry IV* plays against Shakespeare's original intentions. Ned Poins is a kind of minor league Horatio, a yes-man to Hal's Hamlet. Shakespeare did not bother to give Poins a personality. Take him out of the plays and who would notice? Gray legions of routine Shakespeare scholars might still take an interest in the Henriad if Falstaff was banished from it, but try the dismal experiment of the Henriad without the Fat Knight. It would be an elevated version of the *Henry VI* plays.

I stare at the footnotes in the Arden edition of *Henry IV, Part 1* and am informed that Falstaff conceals his cowardice by telling us that discretion is the better part of valor. It meant and means: "the right to choose what should be done in a particular situation." If you are an old fat man desperately fending off the Scottish killing-machine Douglas, you save your life by feigning death. Sometimes I think that scholars condescend to Falstaff, whose cognitive powers far exceed theirs, as a defense against their own cowardice. In any case they seem to wish him dead.

I have long believed that William Shakespeare sensibly turned and ran the other way when violence descended upon the streets of London. He knew that discretion was the better part of valor, a lesson I learned in my far-off youth. Clearly he did not want the first of his great personalities eviscerated, whether by the Earl of Douglas or by the Prince of Wales, who proposes that honor for the sly Sir John, who is shamming death.

Shakespeare will not allow Falstaff to die upon stage. We see and hear the deaths of Hamlet, Cleopatra, Antony, Othello, and

Lear. Iago is led away to die silently under torture. Macbeth dies offstage but he goes down fighting. Falstaff dies singing the Twenty-third Psalm, smiling upon his fingertips, playing with flowers, and crying aloud to God three or four times. That sounds more like pain than prayer.

We do not want Sir John Falstaff to die. And of course he does not. He is life itself. Every other week I lose another friend or good acquaintance to death. My generation passes. It comforts me that Falstaff is among the Everliving.

I bring these surmises back to Falstaff's soliloquy on sherris sack. His sack is heavy oloroso. It operates by ascending into his brain and rendering it responsive, inventive, vehement, and engenders the highest wit. It also warms the blood, lights up the contents, and acts as a beacon calling the kingdom of all of us to arm. The heart is moved to courage and hence Prince Hal is valiant, having been taught by Falstaff to imbibe sack.

We need not literalize Falstaff's sermon. His oloroso is not only pleasant in itself but is the cause of pleasure in those of the Fat Knight's persuasion. Falstaff has lived his faith. He goes into battle at Shrewsbury with a bottle of sack in his holster. A pistol might save his life but his genius is to mock organized violence.

A confirmed bardolator, I nevertheless tire of the monotonous swordplay that is ceaseless in the Histories. Who is up, who is down, is not in itself poetic achievement. None of these puppets ever overhears what he is saying. Falstaff, and to a much lesser degree Hal, change by listening to themselves. Hotspur is glorious and has an intense personality yet he is mindless.

I return to the resurrection of Sir John Falstaff and am aware I quote it the second time in this brief book:

Embowelled? If thou embowel me today, I'll give you leave to powder me, and eat me too, tomorrow. 'Sblood, 'twas time to counterfeit, or that hot termagant Scot had paid me scot and lot too. Counterfeit? I lie, I am no counterfeit: to die, is to be a counterfeit; for he is but the counterfeit of a man who hath not the life of a man: but to counterfeit dying, when a man thereby liveth, is to be no counterfeit, but the true and perfect image of life indeed. The better part of valour is discretion; in the which better part I have saved my life. Zounds, I am afraid of this gunpowder Percy, though he be dead: how, if he should counterfeit too and rise? by my faith, I am afraid he would prove the better counterfeit.

act 5, scene 4, lines 110–23

Earlier Falstaff had admonished Hal: "Never call a true piece of gold a counterfeit." He recalls that and more crucially overhears himself using the word "counterfeit." Everything in me that fights to go on living is heartened by the wisdom of the Socrates of Eastcheap: "to counterfeit dying, when a man thereby liveth, is to be no counterfeit, but the true and perfect image of life indeed."

CHAPTER 17

Master Robert Shallow
and Falstaff

Returning from his easy capture of the feckless Colevile of the
Dale, Falstaff stops to fleece Justice Shallow.

Shallow is absurd yet clear-sighted:

Davy: Doth the man of war stay all night, sir?
Shallow: Yea, Davy. I will use him well: a friend i' the court is
    better than a penny in purse. Use his men well, Davy; for
    they are arrant knaves, and will backbite.
Davy: No worse than they are backbitten, sir; for they have
    marvellous foul linen.
Shallow: Well conceited, Davy: about thy business, Davy.
Davy: I beseech you, sir, to countenance William Visor of
    Woncot against Clement Perkes of the hill.
Shallow: There is many complaints, Davy, against that Visor:
    that Visor is an arrant knave, on my knowledge.
Davy: I grant your worship that he is a knave, sir; but yet, God
    forbid, sir, but a knave should have some countenance at
    his friend's request. An honest man, sir, is able to speak
    for himself, when a knave is not. I have served your
    worship truly, sir, this eight years; and if I cannot once
    or twice in a quarter bear out a knave against an honest
    man, I have but a very little credit with your worship. The

123

knave is mine honest friend, sir; therefore, I beseech your
worship, let him be countenanced.
Shallow: Go to; I say he shall have no wrong. Look about,
Davy.

act 5, scene 1, lines 27–49

The steward Davy is shrewd and witty in response to Shallow's accurate judgment of Falstaff's retainers as complete knaves. Shallow will find no friend at court in Falstaff. Nevertheless he and Davy charm us by their insouciance in regard to justice. The entrance of Falstaff elevates the scene with another grand soliloquy:

I'll follow you, good Master Robert Shallow. [*Exit Shallow.*]
Bardolph, look to our horses. [*Exeunt Bardolph and Page.*] If I
were sawed into quantities, I should make four dozen of such
bearded hermits' staves as Master Shallow. It is a wonderful
thing to see the semblable coherence of his men's spirits and his:
they, by observing of him, do bear themselves like foolish justices; he, by conversing with them, is turned into a justice-like
serving-man: their spirits are so married in conjunction with
the participation of society that they flock together in consent,
like so many wild-geese. If I had a suit to Master Shallow, I
would humour his men with the imputation of being near their
master: if to his men, I would curry with Master Shallow that
no man could better command his servants. It is certain that
either wise bearing or ignorant carriage is caught, as men take
diseases, one of another: therefore let men take heed of their
company. I will devise matter enough out of this Shallow to
keep Prince Harry in continual laughter the wearing out of six
fashions, which is four terms, or two actions, and a' shall laugh
without intervallums. O, it is much that a lie with a slight oath

and a jest with a sad brow will do with a fellow that never had
the ache in his shoulders! O, you shall see him laugh till his face
be like a wet cloak ill laid up!

act 5, scene 1, lines 57–82

This seems to me the most searching of Falstaff's homilies.
Noting the interchange of personalities from master to servant,
Shallow to Davy, Sir John glides over the mutual influence he and
Hal exercise upon each other. Shallow will provide him with a
treasury of laughter to bestow upon the Prince. His own frame
racked with pains and aches, Falstaff approaches resentment of
Hal's youthful vigor.

Beneath the jocular tone shadows cluster. Never again will
Falstaff rouse Hal to the spirit of comedy. Hal's finest moment had
been a soliloquy of sublime wit that reflects the style of Sir John:

> I am not yet of Percy's mind, the Hotspur of the north; he that
> kills me some six or seven dozen of Scots at a breakfast, washes
> his hands, and says to his wife 'Fie upon this quiet life! I want
> work.' 'O my sweet Harry,' says she, 'how many hast thou killed
> to-day?' 'Give my roan horse a drench,' says he; and answers
> 'Some fourteen,' an hour after; 'a trifle, a trifle.' I prithee, call in
> Falstaff: I'll play Percy, and that damned brawn shall play Dame
> Mortimer his wife. 'Rivo!' says the drunkard. Call in ribs, call
> in tallow.

act 2, scene 4, lines 98–108

Here also shadows impend. Hal will play Hotspur and Falstaff,
nastily termed pig meat, will be his wife. One admires the buoyancy of Hal's wit while shuddering at the animosity.

I am moved to an excursus on the value, never to be renewed,
sparked by the language of both men during their earlier relation-

125

ship. Perhaps Falstaff's language is all they ever could have shared. If Hal possessed any authentic affection for Falstaff, Shakespeare does not impart it to us. When he thinks the Fat Knight has been slain by Douglas, the best he can manage is "Poor Jack, farewell." This contrasts with his farewell to Hotspur as a "great heart."

In the past I overestimated Falstaff's affection for Hal. When Sir John enters to find Hal and Hotspur dueling, he reacts ironically and stays to enjoy a spectator's pleasures: "Well said, Hal! To it, Hal! Nay, you shall find no boy's play here, I can tell you." Had Hotspur won, he would next have turned to Falstaff, who knows that would have been his death. Nevertheless, the despised brawn will take his chances.

We are at the cusp of Hal's transmutation into King Henry V and of Falstaff falling into the way down and out. I am perplexed by the insoluble paradox of two antithetical personalities who shared revelry, fellowship, and the invention of a language.

The least interesting aspect of the rejection of Falstaff is Hal's fulfillment by it. More fascinating and disturbing is Falstaff's rejection of Falstaff. Totally immeasurable is what could be termed Shakespeare's rejection of Falstaff. I say that and I am bewildered. Falstaff freed Shakespeare for Hamlet, Lear, Macbeth, and Cleopatra. Why did he end his first great invention?

Returning to the Sonnets, something subtle and self-destructive in the speaker has affinities with Falstaff's ultimately catastrophic friendship with Hal:

Say that thou didst forsake me for some fault,
And I will comment upon that offence;
Speak of my lameness, and I straight will halt,
Against thy reasons making no defence.
Thou canst not, love, disgrace me half so ill,
To set a form upon desired change,

As I'll myself disgrace: knowing thy will,
I will acquaintance strangle and look strange,
Be absent from thy walks, and in my tongue
Thy sweet beloved name no more shall dwell,
Lest I, too much profane, should do it wrong
And haply of our old acquaintance tell.
  For thee against myself I'll vow debate,
  For I must ne'er love him whom thou dost hate.

             Sonnet 89

Katherine Duncan-Jones, in her very useful edition of the Sonnets, astutely notes the possible relation of line 11, "Lest I, too
much profane, should do it wrong," to Henry V's rejection of
Falstaff. In his angry speech of contempt, the newly crowned King
describes Falstaff as "so surfeit-swelled, so old and so profane." The
poet of the Sonnets and Falstaff are both unacceptable in noble
or royal company. The resemblance of poem and play cannot be
taken too far. Could we possibly think of Falstaff as the speaker of
Sonnet 89?

The young nobleman Henry Wriothesley, Earl of Southampton, may be the protagonist of some of the early Sonnets. William Herbert, Earl of Pembroke, appears to be the young man
addressed in the later Sonnets. He was Shakespeare's patron and
generous also to several other poets of that day. Richard Burbage,
Shakespeare's major actor, had a close friendship with Pembroke.
It seems accurate to surmise that Burbage and Ben Jonson were
Shakespeare's best friends.

The Sonnets are the finest in the English language but their
biographical context is all but impossible to definitively ascertain.
Shakespeare seems to have designed his own absence from the
sequence. Interpreting him, one grasps any handhold that can be
found. So unlimited is his span that we are lost and that is our

wonder. Genre distinctions dissolve for him; comedy, history, trag-edy, and so-called romance blend in play after play.

Does Shakespeare reject himself in the Sonnets? Does he reject Falstaff? Yes and no, no and yes. In the Sonnets he takes the side of Pembroke at his own expense. Does Falstaff, as he ebbs away in Eastcheap, blame only himself? That is to choose death over life and to cease being Sir John Falstaff.

CHAPTER 18

Falstaff in Shallow's Orchard

After the death of Henry IV we have our first encounter with Henry V. Doubtless his grief for the dead father is authentic enough, though his address to his uneasy brothers is centered elsewhere:

> This new and gorgeous garment, majesty,
> Sits not so easy on me as you think.
> Brothers, you mix your sadness with some fear:
> This is the English, not the Turkish court;
> Not Amurath an Amurath succeeds,
> But Harry Harry. Yet be sad, good brothers,
> For, by my faith, it very well becomes you:
> Sorrow so royally in you appears
> That I will deeply put the fashion on
> And wear it in my heart: why then, be sad;
> But entertain no more of it, good brothers,
> Than a joint burden laid upon us all.
> For me, by heaven, I bid you be assured,
> I'll be your father and your brother too;
> Let me but bear your love, I'll bear your cares:
> Yet weep that Harry's dead; and so will I;
> But Harry lives, that shall convert those tears
> By number into hours of happiness.
>
> *Henry IV, Part 2*, act 5, scene 2, lines 44–61

The sons of the dead King are a warrior clan and perhaps the only love they can experience is for one another. That includes Henry V, who commences by disowning the Turkish Sultan Murad III, known as Amurath, who murdered all his brothers when he mounted the throne. Star of England as he may have been, the new King is totally ruthless and dedicated to killing to extend and enhance his power. You can be charmed by him in *Henry V* but only if you can shrug off a leader who instructs his soldiers to cut the throats of their French prisoners.

Falstaff's nemesis, the Lord Chief Justice, is embraced by the new King in a stunning speech that warrants considerable analysis:

> You are right, justice, and you weigh this well;
> Therefore still bear the balance and the sword:
> And I do wish your honours may increase,
> Till you do live to see a son of mine
> Offend you and obey you, as I did.
> So shall I live to speak my father's words:
> 'Happy am I, that have a man so bold,
> That dares do justice on my proper son;
> And not less happy, having such a son,
> That would deliver up his greatness so
> Into the hands of justice.' You did commit me:
> For which, I do commit into your hand
> The unstained sword that you have used to bear;
> With this remembrance, that you use the same
> With the like bold, just and impartial spirit
> As you have done 'gainst me. There is my hand.
> You shall be as a father to my youth:
> My voice shall sound as you do prompt mine ear,
> And I will stoop and humble my intents
> To your well-practised wise directions.

And, princes all, believe me, I beseech you;
My father is gone wild into his grave,
For in his tomb lie my affections;
And with his spirit sadly I survive,
To mock the expectation of the world,
To frustrate prophecies and to raze out
Rotten opinion, who hath writ me down
After my seeming. The tide of blood in me
Hath proudly flow'd in vanity till now:
Now doth it turn and ebb back to the sea,
Where it shall mingle with the state of floods
And flow henceforth in formal majesty.
Now call we our high court of parliament:
And let us choose such limbs of noble counsel,
That the great body of our state may go
In equal rank with the best govern'd nation;
That war, or peace, or both at once, may be
As things acquainted and familiar to us;
In which you, father, shall have foremost hand.
Our coronation done, we will accite,
As I before remember'd, all our state:
And, God consigning to my good intents,
No prince nor peer shall have just cause to say,
God shorten Harry's happy life one day!

act 5, scene 2, lines 102–45

Always eloquent, Henry V's tonalities reverberate with royal authority. Ironies beyond his ken hover in his pronouncement. His son Henry VI, anything but a rebel, will neither fight nor flee, as his fierce wife, Margaret of Anjou, complains. I am startled by the superb line, "My father is gone wild into his grave." I do not believe it means that the new King's wildness has been interred with his father, as though all passion is spent. It is Henry IV who departed wild into his grave, forlorn and haggard, his guilt for the murder of Richard II unexpiated.

The new King's voice swells to a tone of royal magnificence as he chants his newfound self-realization:

> The tide of blood in me
> Hath proudly flow'd in vanity till now:
> Now doth it turn and ebb back to the sea,
> Where it shall mingle with the state of floods
> And flow henceforth in formal majesty.
>
> act 5, scene 2, lines 129–33

Henry V flaunts his exuberance as his own intense pride merges with the majesty of the sea. His obsession with "vanity," a perpetual reproach leveled at Falstaff, is at last exorcised. We approach the Warrior King who will lead his nation in an imperialistic crusade to devour France.

Shakespeare is the master of simultaneity. Even as Henry V is coronated, Falstaff and his cohorts are led by Shallow into his orchard. There is a strange beauty in this scene. A kind of aura pervades as we are given a pastoral interlude between Hal's Accession and the downward plummet of Falstaff's entire being. It is as though Shakespeare wants us to linger in an England momentarily at peace. The rebels all have been executed. Henry V's French expedition has not yet been lost. Falstaff lives, dies, lives again, and all but dies again as the Henriad overwhelms the Falstaffiad.

A surprising element in the orchard scene is the sudden emergence of Silence as a merry songster. His first lyric, doubtless of Shakespeare's composition, moves in the atmosphere of old English merriment:

[*Singing*]
Do nothing but eat, and make good cheer,
And praise God for the merry year;
When flesh is cheap and females dear,
And lusty lads roam here and there
     So merrily,
And ever among so merrily.

act 5, scene 3, lines 17–22

Shakespeare's fabled slyness shines forth in that admirable line: "When flesh is cheap and females dear." As a loving Falstaffian, I am heartened by the final epiphany of the Fat Knight at his happiest:

Falstaff: There's a merry heart! Good Master Silence, I'll give you a health for that anon.

Shallow: Give Master Bardolph some wine, Davy.

Davy: Sweet sir, sit; I'll be with you anon; most sweet sir, sit. Master page, good master page, sit. Proface! What you want in meat, we'll have in drink: but you must bear; the heart's all.

[*Exit.*]

Shallow: Be merry, Master Bardolph; and, my little soldier there, be merry.

Silence: [*Singing*] Be merry, be merry, my wife has all;
For women are shrews, both short and tall:
'Tis merry in hall when beards wag all,
And welcome merry Shrove-tide.
Be merry, be merry.

Falstaff: I did not think Master Silence had been a man of this mettle.

There is poignance in this convivial scene, since we know that Falstaff cannot long continue in his vocation. He has been called to a life of laughter and skullduggery, and has won us by his answer to that call:

Silence: Who, I? I have been merry twice and once ere now.
[*Re-enter Davy.*]
Davy: [*To Bardolph*] There's a dish of leather-coats for you.
Shallow: Davy!
Davy: Your worship! I'll be with you straight.
[*To Bardolph*] A cup of wine, sir?
Silence: [*Singing*] A cup of wine that's brisk and fine,
And drink unto thee, leman mine;
And a merry heart lives long-a.
Falstaff: Well said, Master Silence.
Silence: An we shall be merry, now comes in the sweet o' the
    night.
Falstaff: Health and long life to you, Master Silence.
Silence: [*Singing*] Fill the cup, and let it come;
I'll pledge you a mile to the bottom. . . .
[*Knocking within*]
Shallow: Look who's at door there, ho! who knocks?
[*Exit Davy.*]
Falstaff: [*To Silence, seeing him take off a bumper*] Why, now you
    have done me right.
Silence: [*Singing*] Do me right,
And dub me knight: Samingo.
Is't not so?
Falstaff: 'Tis so.
Silence: Is't so? Why then, say an old man can do somewhat.

act 5, scene 3, lines 23–77

Davy, acting as host, cries out "Proface!," or welcome to the feast. Shakespeare appropriates the proverb "what they want in meat let them take and drink" and reminds us that the heart is all. Merriment sweeps through them. Silence sings another of Shakespeare's ditties welcoming Shrove-tide, the festival season that precedes Ash Wednesday and Lent. With great sweetness, Falstaff expresses his wonder at Silence as a man of such capacity for joy. The lovely reply goes to my heart: "Who I? I have been merry twice and once ere now."

As the sack goes round, spirits rise and good fellowship prevails. With exquisite timing Shakespeare gives us one of his ominous knocks on the door. It is Ancient Pistol come from court to proclaim tidings that should be marvelous for Falstaff yet we know will prove catastrophic:

Pistol: Sir John, God save you!
Falstaff: What wind blew you hither, Pistol?
Pistol: Not the ill wind which blows no man to good. Sweet knight, thou art now one of the greatest men in this realm.
Silence: By'r lady, I think a' be, but goodman Puff of Barson.
Pistol: Puff!
Puff in thy teeth, most recreant coward base!
Sir John, I am thy Pistol and thy friend,
And helter-skelter have I rode to thee,
And tidings do I bring and lucky joys
And golden times and happy news of price.
Falstaff: I pray thee now, deliver them like a man of this world.
Pistol: A foutre for the world and worldlings base!
I speak of Africa and golden joys.
Falstaff: O base Assyrian knight, what is thy news?
Let King Cophetua know the truth thereof.

Silence: [*Singing*] And Robin Hood, Scarlet, and John.
Pistol: Shall dunghill curs confront the Helicons?
And shall good news be baffled?
Then, Pistol, lay thy head in Furies' lap.

. . .

Pistol: Sir John, thy tender lambkin now is king;
Harry the Fifth's the man. I speak the truth:
When Pistol lies, do this; and fig me, like
The bragging Spaniard.
Falstaff: What, is the old king dead?
Pistol: As nail in door: the things I speak are just.
Falstaff: Away, Bardolph! saddle my horse. Master Robert
      Shallow, choose what office thou wilt in the land, 'tis
      thine. Pistol, I will double-charge thee with dignities.
Bardolph: O joyful day!
I would not take a knighthood for my fortune.
Pistol: What! I do bring good news.
Falstaff: Carry Master Silence to bed. Master Shallow, my
      Lord Shallow,—be what thou wilt; I am fortune's
      steward—get on thy boots: we'll ride all night. O
      sweet Pistol! Away, Bardolph! Come, Pistol, utter
      more to me; and withal devise something to do thyself
      good. Boot, boot, Master Shallow: I know the young
      king is sick for me. Let us take any man's horses; the
      laws of England are at my commandment. Blessed are
      they that have been my friends; and woe to my lord
      chief-justice!
Pistol: Let vultures vile seize on his lungs also!
'Where is the life that late I led?' say they:
Why, here it is; welcome these pleasant days!
                              act 5, scene 3, lines 82–137

Pistol is Pistolian, ranting and puffing, but achieves a kind of good nonsense with: "I speak of Africa and golden joys." In high style, Falstaff salutes his Ancient as: "O base Assyrian knight," and throws in a ballad a "Beggar and a King," who is Cophetua, a potentate Shakespeare already had invoked in *Love's Labour's Lost*. . . .

Decline and fall, the ebbing away of the Immortal Falstaff, is upon us as Sir John goes wild with that kind of madness the gods bring to us for our self-destruction. I for one suffer as I hear Falstaff proclaim that he is "Fortune's steward." Scholars tell us that Falstaff is not becoming a horse thief. Rather, in Henry V's name, he seizes horses for a purpose supposedly inspired by the state. Total self-annihilation comes with the fearsome declaration "the laws of England are at my commandment." Even the most Falstaffian of audiences would have shuddered at that. Pistol is at his worst in wishing the fate of Prometheus upon the Lord Chief Justice, and then partly redeems himself with a scrap or a tag that Cole Porter employed so well in *Kiss Me, Kate*, "Where is the life that late I led?" The final note is at once acceptable and plangent: "Welcome these pleasant days!"

I stand back from the orchard scene and sorrow descends like rain. Falstaff knows better, how could he not? His keen intellect and deep awareness of Hal's burgeoning ambivalence is negated as he falls into denial. The darkness soon enough will drop and Falstaff will vanish into it. Shakespeare, who owed Falstaff so much, may have felt a regret. But the art of the greatest of poet-playwrights demanded sacrifices. Falstaff goes down so that Hamlet and his successors could live and move and enjoy their being.

CHAPTER 19

The Arrest of Mistress Quickly and Doll Tearsheet

With palpable pleasure Shakespeare inserts between Falstaff's rush to self-annihilation, and the pageant of rejection, a fierce scene in which two beadles, whose office was to whip harlots and make things nasty for other minor offenders, drag in the outraged Mistress Quickly and Doll Tearsheet:

> [*Enter Beadles, dragging in Mistress Quickly and Doll Tearsheet.*]
> **Mistress Quickly:** No, thou arrant knave! I would to God that I might die, that I might have thee hanged. Thou hast drawn my shoulder out of joint.
> **First Beadle:** The constables have delivered her over to me, and she shall have whipping-cheer enough, I warrant her, there hath been a man or two lately killed about her.
> **Doll Tearsheet:** Nut-hook, nut-hook, you lie! Come on, I'll tell thee what, thou damned tripe-visaged rascal, an the child I now go with do miscarry, thou wert better thou hadst struck thy mother, thou paper-faced villain.
> **Mistress Quickly:** O the Lord, that Sir John were come! He would make this a bloody day to somebody. But I pray God the fruit of her womb miscarry!
> **First Beadle:** If it do, you shall have a dozen of cushions again; you have but eleven now. Come, I charge you both go

with me; for the man is dead that you and Pistol beat
amongst you.

Doll Tearsheet: I'll tell you what, you thin man in a censer,
I will have you as soundly swinged for this—you blue-
bottle rogue, you filthy famished correctioner, if you be
not swinged, I'll forswear half-kirtles.

First Beadle: Come, come, you she knight-errant, come!

Mistress Quickly: O God, that right should thus overcome
might! Well, of sufferance comes ease.

Doll Tearsheet: Come, you rogue, come, bring me to a justice.

Mistress Quickly: Ay, come, you starved bloodhound.

Doll Tearsheet: Goodman death, goodman bones!

Mistress Quickly: Thou atomy, thou!

Doll Tearsheet: Come, you thin thing, come you rascal!

First Beadle: Very well.

act 5, scene 4, lines 1–31

Mistress Quickly and Doll Tearsheet superbly harangue the
beadles in unison, clearly showing the influence of Falstaff's language. Doll Tearsheet achieves new heights in reducing the beadle
to a catchpoll or stick to pull down branches. Her plea of pregnancy is one of her standard stratagems for evading the law. Having heard this before, he indicates the ruse is being played for the
twelfth time, the cushions simulating pregnancy. I have my doubts
that Quickly, Tearsheet, and Pistol had beaten any man to death,
as it is most unlikely. Waxing to even grander rant, Doll Tearsheet
calls the blue-clad beadle a correctioner, thus emulating Shakespeare's proclivity for carnage. After she threatens to have a correctioner beaten, she promises to wear no more skirts or in effect
to abandon her ancient profession.

The beadle, thus challenged, meets the occasion by the witty
quibble in which Doll is a night-errant, one who sins at night.

Quickly, ever the malaprop, says the opposite of what she means and then—"of sufferance comes ease"—utters a proverb hopelessly ambiguous.

The two defiant charmers are carried off to what is called justice, chanting delicious insults geared to the walking skeleton who will punish them. We never will see Doll Tearsheet again, which is a pity. Would you rather watch and listen to her or Prince John of Lancaster? Mistress Quickly will return in *King Henry V*, where we will hear her elegizing Falstaff.

The Hal who held together the disparate worlds of warrior-politicians and of Falstaff's Eastcheap no longer exists. We barely recognize him in King Henry V. Doubtless there is gain as well as evident loss. But where is Shakespeare himself in this diminishing into a king?

Since Shakespeare so contains us, so does Falstaff. Sir John will not fit any categories assigned to him. His mystery is akin to what all of us confront in our daily lives. Are we characters, thinkers, or personalities? At eighty-six I have in common with Falstaff the will to live, which sustains me at a dreary time. When Falstaff and his group are carried off to the Fleet for momentary incarceration, how are we to imagine he felt as he lay there in durance? Shakespeare wisely chose not to represent that sadness. I have never been in jail but time in the hospital is notoriously slowed down to stasis. The word "patient" is apt for those who must wait and endure.

CHAPTER 20

The Rejection of Falstaff

Though act 5, scene 5 of *Henry IV, Part 2* is the actual depiction of the new King casting off Falstaff, the entire mingled Henriad and Falstaffiad is nothing but that rejection. This scene is one of Shakespeare's most remarkable achievements. It begins with three grooms who are strewing rushes on the streets to prepare for the arrival of King Henry V and his train. To the sound of trumpets, the King and entourage pass over the stage. Only after them do we see the entrance of Falstaff, attended by Shallow, Pistol, Bardolph, and the Page. Each time I reread or teach the scene I suffer the anticipation of what Falstaff secretly not only expects but courts:

> Falstaff: Stand here by me, Master Robert Shallow, I will
> make the king do you grace. I will leer upon him as a'
> comes by, and do but mark the countenance that he will
> give me.
> Pistol: God bless thy lungs, good knight!
> Falstaff: Come here, Pistol, stand behind me. [*To Shallow*] O,
> if I had had time to have made new liveries, I would have
> bestowed the thousand pound I borrowed of you. But 'tis
> no matter, this poor show doth better, this doth infer the
> zeal I had to see him.
> Shallow: It doth so.
> Falstaff: It shows my earnestness of affection,—
> Shallow: It doth so.

Falstaff: My devotion,—

Shallow: It doth, it doth, it doth.

Falstaff: As it were, to ride day and night, and not to deliberate,
not to remember, not to have patience to shift me,—

Shallow: It is best, certain.

Falstaff: But to stand stained with travel, and sweating with
desire to see him, thinking of nothing else, putting all
affairs else in oblivion, as if there were nothing else to be
done but to see him.

Pistol: 'Tis *semper idem*, for *obsque hoc nihil est*: 'tis all in every
part.

Shallow: 'Tis so, indeed.

Pistol: My knight, I will inflame thy noble liver,

And make thee rage.

Thy Doll, and Helen of thy noble thoughts,

Is in base durance and contagious prison,

Hal'd thither

By most mechanical and dirty hand.

Rouse up Revenge from ebon den with fell Alecto's snake,

For Doll is in. Pistol speaks nought but truth.

Falstaff: I will deliver her. [*Shouts within.*]

[*The trumpets sound.*]

Pistol: There roar'd the sea, and trumpet-clangor sounds.

act 5, scene 5, lines 5–40

The spirit has already abandoned Falstaff. His living and laughing mode of speech is absent. We could be listening to any down-
at-heels, would-be courtier who desperately knows he has no
chance of preferment. Our modern sense of "leer" as naughty or sly
is not valid here. Poor Falstaff intends to look yearningly upon his
former companion in play. The thousand pounds he has extorted

from Shallow may have some reference to the sum granted Shakespeare by the Earl of Southampton. Until 1603 Shakespeare's company were the Lord Chamberlain's Men. Under James I they became the King's Men. Southampton's gift evidently enabled Shakespeare to purchase a full share in the company, upon which his subsequent fortune was to be founded.

It is painful to hear Falstaff stammer his hopeless desire to be accepted by Henry V. When Pistol rants that Doll is in Bridewell, poor Falstaff declares: "I will deliver her." The trumpets sound, the new King enters with the Lord Chief Justice and the rest of his court, and Falstaff plunges into the pit:

> **Falstaff:** God save thy grace, King Hal, my royal Hal!
> **Pistol:** The heavens thee guard and keep, most royal imp of
>   fame!
> **Falstaff:** God save thee, my sweet boy!
> **King Henry V:** My Lord Chief Justice, speak to that vain man.
> **Lord Chief Justice:** Have you your wits? Know you what 'tis
>   you speak?
> **Falstaff:** My King! my Jove! I speak to thee, my heart!
>
> act 5, scene 5, lines 41–46

The fatal word "vain" sounds again to knell the doom of Falstaff. I always startle when Falstaff cries out "My King! my Jove! I speak to thee, my heart!" Sir John is Old Father Time or Cronos, who castrated and usurped his father Uranus. Jove, the son of Cronos, displaced him a touch less violently. Saturn, the Roman name for Cronos, presided over a golden age. Falstaff, superbly intelligent even in his desperation, is highly aware of what he is saying.

Henry V is never more brilliant or cruel than in his powerfully phrased rejection:

I know thee not, old man. Fall to thy prayers;
How ill white hairs become a fool and jester!
I have long dreamt of such a kind of man,
So surfeit-swell'd, so old and so profane;
But, being awak'd I do despise my dream.
Make less thy body hence, and more thy grace;
Leave gormandizing; know the grave doth gape
For thee thrice wider than for other men.
Reply not to me with a fool-born jest:
Presume not that I am the thing I was;
For God doth know, so shall the world perceive,
That I have turn'd away my former self;
So will I those that kept me company.
When thou dost hear I am as I have been,
Approach me, and thou shalt be as thou wast,
The tutor and the feeder of my riots.
Till then, I banish thee, on pain of death,
As I have done the rest of my misleaders,
Not to come near our person by ten mile.
For competence of life I will allow you,
That lack of means enforce you not to evils;
And, as we hear you do reform yourselves,
We will, according to your strengths and qualities,
Give you advancement.
[*To the Lord Chief Justice*] Be it your charge, my lord,
To see perform'd the tenor of my word.
Set on.

act 5, scene 5, lines 47–72

"I know thee not, old man." In one sense, the King means he no longer knows Falstaff; in another, that he never knew him. The pious monarch urges Sir John to kneel down and pray. A former companion is now only a fool and jester, a figure of dream. The awakened Henry V loathes that dream, as we do not. For a single moment we hear Hal, in the playful jest that the grave beckons Falstaff thrice wider as Sir John is three times normal weight. Hastily the King stops Falstaff from joking in return, with the odious line "Presume not that I am the thing I was."

Shakespeare was well aware of the sanctimonious pomposity of Henry V saying that God knows and the world will soon perceive that the Prodigal Son has reformed. But Falstaff is banished at least ten miles away, which may indicate an uneasiness. Rather grudgingly, Sir John will be allowed a stipend lest he turn to highway robbery again. There is a sinister clash between the absurd promise that an improved Falstaff will receive advancement, and the grim charge to the Lord Chief Justice to see the royal word performed.

There is a personal Shakespearean overtone in: "Master Shallow, I owe you a thousand pound." Poor Shallow beseeches repayment to no avail and achieves some wit in response:

Shallow: I cannot well perceive how, unless you should give me your doublet and stuff me out with straw. I beseech you, good Sir John, let me have five hundred of my thousand.

Falstaff: Sir, I will be as good as my word: this that you heard was but a colour.

Shallow: A colour that I fear you will die in, Sir John.

Falstaff: Fear no colours: go with me to dinner: come, Lieutenant Pistol; come, Bardolph: I shall be sent for soon at night.

act 5, scene 5, lines 81–90

By "colour" Falstaff means a pretense, to which Shallow rejoins with a double pun "colour" and "collar" or the noose, and "dye" or "die." A final pathos is heard in "I shall be sent for soon at night," which Sir John does not believe. Instead, the Lord Chief Justice and Prince John of Lancaster, both fixed enemies of Falstaff, enter with officers and command Sir John and everyone with him to be carried to the Fleet prison. The last words we will ever hear from Falstaff are his desperate "My lord, my lord,—." It is a sorry departure for the world's most substantial wit.

I have already commented on Sonnet 89, "Say that thou didst forsake me for some fault." The two flanking Sonnets, 88 and 90, also may be relevant to the rejection of Falstaff:

When thou shalt be disposed to set me light
And place my merit in the eye of scorn,
Upon thy side against myself I'll fight,
And prove thee virtuous, though thou art forsworn.
With mine own weakness being best acquainted,
Upon thy part I can set down a story
Of faults concealed, wherein I am attainted,
That thou in losing me shalt win much glory.
And I by this will be a gainer too,
For bending all my loving thoughts on thee,
The injuries that to myself I do,
Doing thee vantage, double vantage me.
    Such is my love, to thee I so belong,
    That for thy right myself will bear all wrong.

Sonnet 88

Then hate me when thou wilt; if ever, now;
Now, while the world is bent my deeds to cross,
Join with the spite of fortune, make me bow,
And do not drop in for an after-loss.
Ah, do not, when my heart hath 'scaped this sorrow,

Come in the rearward of a conquer'd woe;
Give not a windy night a rainy morrow,
To linger out a purposed overthrow.
If thou wilt leave me, do not leave me last,
When other petty griefs have done their spite;
But in the onset come; so shall I taste
At first the very worst of fortune's might;
    And other strains of woe, which now seem woe,
    Compared with loss of thee will not seem so.

Sonnet 90

Shakespeare's rejection by William Herbert, Earl of Pembroke, has a sexual element absent from the Hal-Falstaff relationship. What matters is rejection. It is a common sorrow for all of us whether it costs us a lover or a friend. Shakespeare abounds in rejections. Hamlet viciously casts off Ophelia and thus provokes her suicide. Othello rejects Iago as his second-in-command, a devastation that strikes at Iago's fundamental being. *The Tragedy of King Lear* turns on the King's casting-off of his beloved daughter Cordelia and on the Earl of Gloucester's repudiation of his true son Edgar.

I would not venture that what may have been Shakespeare's own sorrow of rejection influenced Hamlet, Lear, Othello. Yet we know the full depths of our own rejections by apprehending Shakespeare's insights. Falstaff, haunted by the parable of Dives and Lazarus, may reflect Shakespeare's own meditation upon that harshest of all the pronouncements of Jesus. We cannot know.

The rejection of Falstaff, whether or not Shakespeare shared in it, is a rejection of our own will to live. For me and for many others, Falstaff bears the Blessing. Henry V had not the power to withdraw that Blessing.

CHAPTER 21

The Death of
Sir John Falstaff

All of *King Henry V*, from my perspective, could be called *The Death of Sir John Falstaff*. Yet, as I have said, Shakespeare will not let us see him die.

One might call Falstaff's relation to *King Henry V* the Real Absence. His aura hovers throughout.

The doomed survivors of Sir John's band of irregular humorists gather together in the street near the Boar's Head Tavern to engage in their mimic quarrels. The widowed Nell Quickly surprisingly has married the egregious Pistol, thus jilting Nym, a scalawag whose name means "thief."

> **Nym:** Will you shog off? I would have you *solus*.
> **Pistol:** *Solus*, egregious dog? O viper vile!
> The *solus* in thy most mervailous face,
> The *solus* in thy teeth, and in thy throat,
> And in thy hateful lungs, yea, in thy maw, perdy,
> And, which is worse, within thy nasty mouth!
> I do retort the *solus* in thy bowels,
> For I can take, and Pistol's cock is up,
> And flashing fire will follow. . . .
> **Nym:** I will cut thy throat one time or other, in fair terms, that
> is the humour of it.

Pistol: 'Couple a gorge!'
That is the word. I thee defy again.
O hound of Crete, think'st thou my spouse to get?
No, to the spital go,
And from the powdering-tub of infamy
Fetch forth the lazar kite of Cressid's kind,
Doll Tearsheet she by name, and her espouse.
I have, and I will hold, the quondam Quickly
For the only she; and *pauca*, there's enough.
Go to.

act 2, scene 1, lines 45–81

Nym challenges Pistol to shog off and thus march with him to a death-duel. Defiantly the ranting Pistol employs false French for throat-cutting and insults Nym as a Cretan hound akin to Actaeon's hunting dogs that turned and destroyed him. A spital or lazar house adds to the rancorous defiance, culminating in Nym's dispatch to the powdering-tub of infamy where you sweat away venereal disease in a cloud of mercury. Cressid who deserted Troilus for Diomede in Chaucer's *Troilus and Criseyde*, and subsequently was punished with leprosy by the gods, is associated with poor Doll Tearsheet, the last mention we will hear of that boisterous spirit.

Pauca is the Latin for "a few," here words, as Pistol concludes. The impending violence is held off by the Boy:

Boy: Mine host Pistol, you must come to my master, and
you, hostess. He is very sick, and would to bed. Good
Bardolph, put thy face between his sheets, and do the
office of a warming-pan. Faith, he's very ill.
Bardolph: Away, you rogue!
Mistress Quickly: By my troth, he'll yield the crow a pudding

one of these days. The King has killed his heart. Good husband, come home presently.

act 2, scene 1, lines 83–89

Since a pudding was meat minced and tied in a skin, Mistress Quickly primly fears that Falstaff will soon be so much carrion. Sir John is yielding either to the plague or syphilis and not to his broken heart:

> **Mistress Quickly:** As ever you come of women, come in quickly to Sir John. Ah, poor heart, he is so shaked of a burning quotidian tertian that it is most lamentable to behold. Sweet men, come to him.
> **Nym:** The King hath run bad humours on the knight, that's the even of it.
> **Pistol:** Nym, thou hast spoke the right;
> His heart is fracted and corroborate.
> **Nym:** The King is a good king, but it must be as it may. He passes some humours and careers.

act 2, scene 1, lines 117–26

Ancient Pistol resorts to Latinisms with "fracted" for "broken" and a misused "corroborate," which means "strengthened" rather than "diminished." The iconic Nym turns to horsemanship where passing a career is to gallop at full speed. King Henry V cannot be turned from riding the horse of his will.

Falstaff has died.

> **Mistress Quickly:** Prithee, honey-sweet husband, let me bring thee to Staines.
> **Pistol:** No; for my manly heart doth earn.

153

Bardolph, be blithe. Nym, rouse thy vaunting veins.

Boy, bristle thy courage up;

For Falstaff he is dead, and we must earn therefore.

Bardolph: Would I were with him, wheresome'er he is, either in heaven or in hell!

Mistress Quickly: Nay, sure, he's not in hell; he's in Arthur's bosom, if ever man went to Arthur's bosom. A' made a finer end, and went away an it had been any christom child. A' parted even just between twelve and one, even at the turning o'th' tide. For after I saw him fumble with the sheets and play wi'th' flowers, and smile upon his fingers' ends, I knew there was but one way; for his nose was as sharp as a pen, and 'a table of green fields. 'How now, Sir John?' quoth I, 'what, man! be o' good cheer.' So a' cried out 'God, God, God!' three or four times. Now I, to comfort him, bid him a' should not think of God; I hoped there was no need to trouble himself with any such thoughts yet. So a' bade me lay more clothes on his feet. I put my hand into the bed and felt them, and they were as cold as any stone. Then I felt to his knees, and so up'ard and up'ard, and all was as cold as any stone.

Nym: They say he cried out of sack.

Mistress Quickly: Ay, that a' did.

Bardolph: And of women.

Mistress Quickly: Nay, that a' did not.

Boy: Yes, that a' did, and said they were devils incarnate.

Mistress Quickly: A' could never abide carnation, 'twas a colour he never liked.

Boy: A' said once the devil would have him about women.

Mistress Quickly: A' did in some sort, indeed, handle women; but then he was rheumatic and talked of the Whore of Babylon.

Boy: Do you not remember a' saw a flea stick upon Bardolph's
nose, and a' said it was a black soul burning in hell-fire?

Bardolph: Well, the fuel is gone that maintained that fire;
that's all the riches I got in his service.

act 2, scene 3, lines 1–42

To "earn" is to "mourn." A variant of "yearn," this grieving is
authentic. Bardolph gives the ultimate tribute to Falstaff: where-
soever Sir John has gone, Bardolph would be there with him. Mistress Quickly follows with her poignant and extraordinary account
of how Falstaff died. The parable of Dives and Lazarus, where the
wretched leper found a final place in Abraham's bosom, is altered
to Arthur's bosom. Snatches of Arthurian ballads seem always to
have been in Falstaff's voice in his prime.

Nell Quickly sees the dying Falstaff as a newly christened baby
and catches the moment of his departure as between twelve and
one even as the Thames ebbed. Fumbling with the bed sheets, Sir
John played with the flowers thrown on them to sweeten the sick-
room. I have seen old friends die with their face falling away and
the nose protruding.

As he dies Falstaff babbles Psalm 23:

A Psalm of David.

1 The Lord is my shepherd, I shall not want.

2 He maketh me to rest in green pasture, and leadeth me by
the still waters.

3 He restoreth my soul, and leadeth me in the paths of righ-
teousness for his Name's sake.

4 Yea, though I should walk through the valley of the shadow
of death, I will fear no evil; for thou art with me: thy rod and thy
staff, they comfort me.

5 Thou dost prepare a table before me in the sight of mine adversaries: thou dost anoint mine head with oil, and my cup runneth over.

6 Doubtless kindness and mercy shall follow me all the days of my life, and I shall remain a long season in the house of the Lord.

Geneva Bible 1599

Nell Quickly, as is her wont, garbles "babbled" with "table." Sweetly she tried to cheer the old reprobate even as he cries out "God, God, God!" That sounds more like a cry of pain than a prayer. Dying, Falstaff begs for more covers even as his legs turn icy. Nell Quickly feels his feet and then up to his knees and then to his testicles and all was as cold as a stone. Subtly Shakespeare alludes to the death of Socrates at the close of Plato's *Phaedo*. Socrates drinks the poison, walks until his legs are numb, and lies down. The poisoner pinches his foot but the sage no longer feels his legs. Just before dying Socrates speaks his final words to Crito: "Crito, we owe a rooster to Asclepius. Please, don't forget to pay the debt."

A soft interpretation would be that Asclepius, the god who cures illnesses, now frees the soul of Socrates from the body. I incline to the interpretation of Robin Waterfield, in his study *Why Socrates Died: Dispelling the Myths*, who intimates that the sage voluntarily chose to be a scapegoat.

It may be that Falstaff, as he neared the end, chose to be a scapegoat, though hardly a cure, for England's malaise. I could indulge the fantasy that Shakespeare, in killing Falstaff, knew he might be killing something in himself. *Henry IV, Part 1* was composed in close sequence to *The Merchant of Venice*. Shylock is hardly a voluntary scapegoat, but that becomes his role.

It is difficult to remember that Shylock inhabits a romantic comedy where he has no place. Falstaff is also out of place in Shakespeare's dramas of history. The speaker of the Sonnets mounts above his rank and then is similarly cast down.

When Nym says that the dying Falstaff cried out against sack, and Bardolph that Sir John cried out against women, Nell Quickly concedes the first but not the second. The Boy heard Falstaff call women devils incarnate and Mistress Quickly gives us the malaprop of Sir John unable to bear the pink color of carnation. The only devils in Shakespeare are human monsters like Iago, Edmund, and Macbeth. Again the Hostess blunders by saying that Falstaff was rheumatic, by which she means delirious, and that he spoke of the Whore of Babylon:

And the woman was arrayed in purple and scarlet, and gilded with gold, and precious stones, and pearls, and had a cup of gold in her hand full of abomination, and filthiness of her fornication.

And in her forehead *was* a name written, A mystery, that great Babylon that mother of whoredoms, and abominations of the earth.

Revelation: 17: 4–5, Geneva Bible 1599

Once Falstaff would have parodied apocalyptic speculations. To repudiate sack and fornication is no longer to be Sir John Falstaff.

Shakespeare uses the word "nothing" about five hundred times in his work. Frequently it is slang for the vagina, as is "hell." Cyril Tourneur in *The Revenger's Tragedy*, certainly his and not Thomas Middleton's, speaks of: "the poor benefit of a bewildering minute."

Why deviate into this darkness in meditating upon the death of Sir John Falstaff? On his deathbed his eros is crucified. Shakespeare wrote *Henry IV, Part 1* when he was thirty-three, the Christological age. In many ways it was his annunciation as a dramatist. Falstaff's emergence may have startled even Shakespeare. When I reflect upon Falstaff one of William Blake's Proverbs of Hell leaps into my mind: "The road of excess leads to the palace of wisdom."

Falstaff and Cleopatra are rammed with life. "Exuberance is Beauty" is another Blakean Proverb of Hell. Hamlet's exuberance of being becomes profoundly negative. Falstaff is his own Hamlet. Hamlet is his own Falstaff. The cry of the human at its most intense emanates from all three.

Falstaff stands between Cleopatra and Hamlet. She refuses to yield and is transfigured by her suicide. Hamlet welcomes death. Falstaff diminishes and dies in misery. And yet the Immortal Falstaff retains his vitality, unmatched in all of Western imaginative literature.

In his glory Sir John Falstaff expresses his credo:

I like not such grinning honour as Sir Walter hath: give me life: which if I can save, so; if not, honour comes unlooked for, and there's an end.

act 5, scene 3, lines 60–62

ABOUT THE AUTHOR

Harold Bloom is Sterling Professor of Humanities at Yale University and a former Charles Eliot Norton Professor at Harvard. His more than forty books include *The Anxiety of Influence*, *The Western Canon*, *Shakespeare: The Invention of the Human*, *The American Religion*, *How to Read and Why*, *Stories and Poems for Extremely Intelligent Children of All Ages*, and *The Daemon Knows*. He is a member of the American Academy of Arts and Letters, a MacArthur Fellow, and the recipient of many awards and honorary degrees, including the American Academy's Gold Medal for Belles Lettres and Criticism, the Hans Christian Andersen Award, the Catalonia International Prize, and the Alfonso Reyes International Prize of Mexico.